This book was found in the breast of my dear son, enveloped with his military sash. Another evidence that he found no difficulty in reconciling devotion to his country, with the duty he owed his God. —

Newburgh, NY
Oct. 10th 1861.

WILL YOU CONSIDER THE SUBJECT

OF

Personal Religion?

Luther in the Convent at Erfurt. p. 218.

The Great Question:

WILL YOU CONSIDER THE SUBJECT OF PERSONAL RELIGION?

By HENRY A. BOARDMAN, D.D.

Philadelphia:
AMERICAN SUNDAY-SCHOOL UNION,
No. 316 CHESTNUT STREET.
NEW YORK: No. 147 NASSAU ST......*BOSTON:* No. 9 CORNHILL.
LOUISVILLE: No. 103 FOURTH ST.
1855

☞ *No books are published by the* AMERICAN SUNDAY-SCHOOL UNION *without the sanction of the Committee of Publication, consisting of fourteen members, from the following denominations of Christians, viz. Baptist, Methodist, Congregational, Episcopal, Presbyterian, Lutheran, and Reformed Dutch. Not more than three of the members can be of the same denomination, and no book can be published to which any member of the Committee shall object.*

PREFACE.

It is an every-day occurrence, to meet with persons who "feel no interest" in the subject of religion, and who, on this ground, excuse themselves from giving their attention to it. I have in very many instances wanted some suitable book to place in the hands of persons of this description.

Within a certain broad and comprehensive sphere, Baxter's Call, Alliene's Alarm, Doddridge's Rise and Progress, or Halyburton's Great Concern of Salvation, might answer the purpose. But, with a great number of individuals, not one of these admirable works could be used with any hope of its being read.

Had I known where to find a book to meet the case, the present volume would not have been written. It has grown out of a conscious and urgent want.

That it will fully supply this acknowledged and serious deficiency in our practical religious literature, I do not allow myself to believe. But I hope it may prove an acceptable offering to some who are either neglecting their own duty, or who have friends to whom they would like to propose the question—"WILL YOU CONSIDER THE SUBJECT OF PERSONAL RELIGION?"

With these views, the work is sent to the press, and humbly commended to HIS blessing, who alone can make it an instrument of good.

H. A. B.

TABLE OF CONTENTS.

SECTION I.

The Great Question.—Will you consider the subject of personal religion?

SECTION II.

Illusive pleas examined.

SECTION III.

The pretexts for neglecting religion, irrational and sordid.

SECTION IV.

Encouragements.

SECTION V.

Religion must and will be considered.

SECTION VI.

What can I do?

The Great Question:

WILL YOU CONSIDER THE SUBJECT OF PERSONAL RELIGION?

I CALLED once upon a very intelligent professional gentleman, for the purpose of conversing with him on the subject of religion. I knew that he had received an excellent Christian education; and that his whole life had been one of exemplary morality. But he was not yet a communicant in the church; and I was anxious to learn the precise ground he occupied.

After stating my errand in general terms, I took occasion to assure him of the interest I felt in his spiritual welfare, and of the satisfaction it would afford me, to see him giving his personal attention to the requirements of the gospel, and identifying himself with its professed disciples. He heard me with something more than respectful courtesy, and when I paused, replied substantially as follows:—

"I feel grateful to you for your kindness in coming to me on this errand. I cordially assent to all you have said on the great importance of personal religion. I wish from my heart I felt the interest in it which you have described. I know this *ought* to be the case, and trust the time is coming when it will be. But as a matter of fact, I must candidly say to you, that I feel no such interest in the subject at present."

"I highly appreciate," I responded, "the frankness of your answer; it is what I should have expected from your training, and your known principles. I am aware, too, of the serious nature of the impediment in your way. It *is* a difficult matter to take up a subject and examine it about which one feels no particular concern, and to which there may even be a conscious antipathy. But religion is of such paramount moment, and the consequences of neglecting it are so irreparable, that neither this nor any other obstacle should hinder us from attending to it. Are you willing to *read* on the subject, and to do other things which may be adapted to inspire you with that interest in it, the want of which you are deploring?"

To this he readily assented. I suggested some books for his perusal, and, with a few counsels, left him. It is not for man always to trace out the subtle mechanism of causes and effects. Nor do I know what agency, or whether any, this interview may have had in the subsequent result. But it is my happiness to know, that this able and estimable man, not very long afterward, made a profession of religion, and has now been for several years a most active and efficient Christian minister, consistent in his life, abundant in his labours, and eminently useful.

This is by no means a solitary example of the kind. Many an individual occupying the same ground with my friend, has, by a similar process, been put in possession of a sure and comfortable hope of eternal life. Very many others there are, who are neglecting their salvation, purely on the ground that they "feel too little interest" in the matter, to take it up; too little even to be willing to examine the gracious offers of the Gospel. It is this class of persons to whom I beg to propose the question: "WILL YOU CONSIDER THE SUBJECT OF PERSONAL RELIGION?" That we may perfectly understand each other, let me define what I suppose to be your state of mind.

You receive Christianity as a divine system. You assent to its teachings. You admit the great alternative it presents, of faith and repentance, or perdition. You go with more or less regularity to the sanctuary. You honour those who show themselves to be real Christians. You hope one day to be among them, but you are not ready for this now. You "feel no particular interest in the subject;" and when it is pressed upon you, you fall back upon this state of indifference, as supplying a reason why you should pass all such appeals over to your neighbours, instead of appropriating them to yourselves. You expect some day to feel the interest in religion which you at present lack, and then you will bestow upon it that careful consideration which it demands. Till that time comes, you must be excused.

Now if this be a just conception of the matter, you cannot fail to see that it brings you within the full sweep of the penalties denounced in the Scriptures against inconsideration. It is no answer to this charge to plead the "want of a disposition" to consider the subject. If you should submit a certain scheme of business or domestic policy to your children, and require their instant attention to it, you would be quite indignant should they treat it with neglect, and then tell you, by way of apology, that they "felt no interest" in examining it. In your view, there would be two sufficient reasons why they should have examined it without delay. First, because of its intrinsic importance; and secondly, because you wished and commanded it. You would regard these considerations as paramount and controlling; as absolutely barring all objections on their part, to a compliance with your instructions. Their predisposition to neglect the matter might even, if foreseen, have been a motive with you for urging it upon them; and what they offered as a palliation of their remissness, might, in your judgment, add to its criminality.

Deal honestly, and apply this reasoning to the case we have in hand. You will not impugn the plenary right of the Deity to submit to us any subject, or prescribe to us any course of conduct he may see fit; and enjoin our immediate attention to it. Should a personage, claiming to have a message for you from God, and exhibiting competent credentials, present himself to you, your feeling would be, that every thing else must give way to this interview; that to subject the ambassador to a moment's unnecessary delay, would be an insult to his master; that whenever and howsoever it was God's pleasure to speak to you, it was your indispensable duty to hear and to obey. But God has spoken to you. He is speaking to you daily. He is speaking not only by prophets and apostles duly accredited, but by his beloved Son. His communication is in your hands. It is in a tongue you can understand. You have access to it every hour of your life. It is, at stated intervals, set forth in your hearing.

You cannot but know what the substance of it is. Will it, therefore, avail you any thing to plead that you have neglected it because you had "no disposition" to consider it? If your obligation to attend to it had been suspended on your state of feeling, this might avail. But there is no such contingency in the case. It was not in ignorance of your state of mind that the message was sent. He who sees the end from the beginning foreknew precisely how you would be situated, and how you would feel; but he did not suppress nor modify the message. He has caused it to be laid before you in its integrity, and demands your candid, thorough, and prayerful consideration of it as your prime duty—a duty which must take precedence of all your secular plans and purposes whatsoever.

It is a mere evasion of this claim, to

urge that you will give your attention to it when you feel "more inclined" to think of it; an evasion which if attempted toward you by your children, would bring down upon them your swift displeasure. In one aspect, it is even a worse affront to God than a positive rejection of the message; for it is a refusal to obey, coupled with a full acknowledgment of his authority to command. You admit that it is God who speaks to you, and yet you will not consider what he says. With what pungent significancy might he say to you, "If I be a father, where is mine honour? and if I be a master, where is my fear?"

Take another view of the ground you occupy. The absolute right of the Supreme Being to propound any theme whatsoever, for your examination, has been conceded. It may aid you in estimating the guilt of your inconsideration, to reflect on the *import* of the communication he has actually submitted to you. Not to launch forth here upon a boundless sea, let it suffice to say, that the BIBLE contains the only adequate revelation of the character and will of God, and discloses the only path which leads from earth to heaven. If our reason and consciences were in a healthful condition, it would startle us, should we ever be conscious of an indisposition to think of Him who made us, and in whom we live and move, and have our being. For what can be more rational, what more unavoidable, one might almost say, than that an intelligent creature should love to think of its Creator? And yet this is one part of the very sin here laid at the door of those with whom we are arguing—an aversion to think of God.

Meditations upon his attributes, especially his moral attributes, are unwelcome to you. You have a tacit compact with yourself, that this subject is to be shunned whenever it *can* be; and so, instead of sitting down to dwell upon the holiness, the justice, the love, and the mercy of the Deity, it is a grateful relief to you on the Sabbath, when the benediction dismisses you from the sanctuary, and you can go where you will not be compelled to hear about God. Surely there must have been some fearful dislocation of your moral faculties, when the essential instincts of your nature are thus overborne, and you can breathe freely only in an atmosphere surcharged with atheism.

To recur to our illustration, what would you think of a group of children, who did their best to *forget* a wise and affectionate father; who drew their daily support from his bounty, without ever thanking him; who availed themselves of his protection when in danger, and experienced his sympathy in sickness and sorrow, without acknowledging his goodness; who rarely mentioned his name in their domestic intercourse, unless it was to point a jest or energize an oath; who, if they could avoid it, would not even permit their minds to dwell upon him, and when they heard others celebrate his virtues, found it a wearisome and stupid theme, to be entertained only so long as good breeding might require? Could an example of this sort be found among the households around you, you well know how notorious it would soon become as an illustration of the blackest filial impiety; how those unnatural children would be pointed at as a set of monsters; and how their names would awaken emotions of horror in every generous bosom.

But what are *you* doing? Have you not a FATHER, wise, bountiful, affectionate; who supplies your daily bread, clothes you, guards you, heals you, comforts you, never wearies in doing you good, never ceases opening to you fresh sources of enjoyment? If so, you at least, who are so indignant at the display of ingratitude and hardihood we have just been contemplating, are earnest and constant in rendering to your Father the love and the homage which are his due. His name is often on your lips. His ear often drinks in the accents of praise which you pour forth on your bended knees. The book which reveals him is your most delightful study. Those who love and honour him most are your favourite companions. The Sabbath is the choicest day of the seven, because it brings the most leisure for communion with him. And you would rather be a door-keeper in his house than to dwell in the tents of wickedness. *Is* it thus with you? Alas! how humiliating the reflection that it may be in all things the very reverse; that even with such a Father you make no suitable return of gratitude; own him not in your business, nor in your family; rarely open his word; seldom, if ever, utter his name; have no love for his ordinances; find his Sabbaths a burden, and repel the very thought of him from your breast, when it seeks to return after you have accomplished the perfunctory routine of public worship! What estimate, in all honesty, ought you to put upon *this* conduct? And what dimensions will you assign to the flagrancy of that *inconsideration* which makes you shun all serious thoughts of God?

Marvellous as this phenomena must appear, there is another no way inferior to it. The inconsideration which the Bible lays at your door has respect no less to *your own character* than to God. It might be supposed, that if an intelligent creature could, under the pressure of some strange mental or moral obliquity, live in the practical forgetfulness of the Being who made him, it would at least be impossible for him to avoid thinking much about himself and his own paramount relations and prospects. It would be taken for granted that every thing pertaining to himself would awaken his deepest interest, and be made the subject of earnest study, just in proportion as it might bear with more or less urgency upon his happiness.

Now, it must certainly be conceded, that you do think much about yourself. The very neglect of God, of which we have just spoken, is combined with an enthronement of self in the heart, and around this centre all the plans of life are made to revolve. Instead of living for God, you live for yourself. His claims are adjourned that your own may be honoured.

And yet it may be true that you are guilty of an extreme and highly criminal inconsideration as regards yourself. It may be that the things concerning yourself, which engross your attention, are stamped with utter insignificance when compared with other things which you neglect. It may be that having (as we all have) two distinct classes of attributes and two sets of relations, the inferior and transitory of these series so monopolizes your care, that you have neither leisure nor inclination to look after the other. At once mortal and immortal, dying and yet deathless, is it not the case, that the personal objects which occupy you are objects all of which are bounded by the narrow horizon of the present life?

Claim for these objects whatever magnitude you may; set forth in whatsoever terms their intrinsic value, and the reasonableness, and even necessity, of pursuing them; expatiate on the importance and obligation of a man's providing for his family, and giving diligent heed to his business, and on the fitness of those social relaxations in which you are accustomed to indulge. Every thing you can equitably demand on these points will be conceded, and you will still be compelled to acknowledge that all these interests are "of the earth, earthy," and that they are no more to be ranked with *other* interests you have, than the body with the soul, and time with eternity.

Is there no room here for the charge of culpable neglect? Is it a calumny to intimate, that among those into whose hands this book may fall, there may be some individual who rarely devotes an hour's serious consideration to the wants, the perils, and the duties of his spiritual nature? You understand well your relations to the world, but when have you investigated your relations with God? You are at home on every question pertaining to your secular engagements, but what do you know in respect to the state of your soul? You keep pace with the progress of public affairs, and scan the journals of every day with eager curiosity to learn what is happening in Washington and in London, at St. Petersburg and Canton; but what progress are you making in self-knowledge, and how much time do you bestow upon the current of events within your own bosom—those events which will affect you for good or for evil, millions of ages after this globe, with its cities and empires, shall have been burned up?

Is it not a most surprising exhibition of inconsideration, that an individual should rarely, if ever, commune with his own heart? That he should know more of what is passing on the opposite side of the globe than of his own real condition? That he should actually spend more time in studying the character and career of some foreign scholar, soldier, or usurper, than he does in examining his own principles and ascertaining his duties and prospects?

This were strange enough, if it could be set down to the account of constitutional levity, or assigned to the category of mere fortuitous results, such as in other departments diversify the tapestry of human life, without having any very tangible causes. But it assumes a more serious aspect, when it is found that the parties in question practise this self-neglect of set purpose; that theirs is a *considerate* inconsideration; that they refrain from looking into their own hearts on system and from absolute aversion. This appears such a crime against the rational nature the Creator has endowed us with, that the statement would be deemed incredible, if the proofs of it were not too incontrovertible to be resisted.

There are, on every side of us, persons whom neither argument nor entreaty can prevail upon to enter into a close and searching scrutiny of their own breasts. They are perfectly aware that they have a long and very grave account with God; but they have no wish to know how it stands. They are conscious that they must die, and that they may die at any moment; but they have no wish to meet the question, "Am I prepared for death?" They are anticipating an endless existence beyond the grave; but they are unwilling to turn their eyes inward long enough to learn whether it is everlasting glory or eternal shame for which they are ripening. There is a something there which repels them. They cannot bear to hold fellowship with themselves. They would sooner look anywhere than into their own hearts. Questions of trade interest them; questions of politics, of science, of literature; the trivial incidents of every-day life; the interchanges of friendship; for all these they have an eye and an ear. But when it comes to inquiries like these: "What am I? Where am I? Whither am I tending? What portion has my soul? How can I meet my God?" all their interest vanishes. They drive out these topics from their breasts as they would a set of intrusive visitors from their houses, and replace them with the evanescent, but more grateful themes which are clothed with the tinsel livery of earth.

An impartial judge would be apt to say, on this naked showing of facts, that there must be something radically wrong here. And, to deal frankly, does it not strike *you* so also—you, I mean, who are implicated in this representation? Admitting, as you do, the existence of all those relations of which we have been speaking, you cannot but regard it as an evil omen that you should be conscious of an indisposition to reflect on your own course of life, to weigh your motives, to explore the recesses of your heart, and learn what manner of spirit you are of. There must be, underneath this superficial complacency of demeanour, a latent feeling that things are not with you as they should be. You are probably no stranger to the misgivings of the merchant who fears to make out a balance-sheet, lest it may prove him a bankrupt; or the misgivings of an invalid, who shrinks from consulting a physician, because he believes himself smitten with a fatal malady. But however that may be, these secret apprehensions are held in check, and you live on in a voluntary ignorance of yourself, which would excite universal wonder, if the depravity which produces it were not also universal.

My object in presenting these considerations is, to lead you to reflect with calmness and impartiality on the position you occupy. The charge the Scriptures bring against you is, that *you will not consider;* that while the beasts of the field, even the least sagacious of them, the ox and the ass, act in accordance with the laws of their constitution, you live in the violation of those laws; that the subjects to which your inconsideration applies are of no mere speculative character, but pre-eminently practical and important; that you are even unwilling to think seriously of your Creator, and what is yet more surprising, to think seriously of yourself.

The impression which such an exposition is adapted to make upon your mind will be still further confirmed, when you remember that this inconsideration, this unwillingness to reflect and investigate, extends to the whole subject of RELIGION. It is not improbable that your associations with this very word may be disagreeable, or at least unwelcome. Against religion in the abstract you have nothing to say. You assent to its teachings. You respect its institutions. You desire its prosperity. You attend, not without some interest, upon its public ministrations. But when it comes to be a personal matter, to the reading of a religious book, to a religious conversation with a Christian friend, to pray, to any thing which looks directly to *your* becoming religious, then your aversion to it begins to work.

If on entering a room alone you should see a table covered with books, and on taking one of them up should find it a religious treatise, would you not lay it down with an emotion almost amounting to positive antipathy? Should you happen to sit down at the same table, with an open Bible before you, would not the first sound of an approaching footstep make you shut up the volume and move from the place, lest perchance some one might suspect you of reading the Scriptures? Or, to proceed a step further, should your pastor call to converse with you on the subject of religion, would you not, if possible, elude either the interview or the subject? Would you not decline a walk with a Christian friend, if you thought he might avail himself of the opportunity to address you in a serious and pointed way on the question of your salvation? Would it not be distasteful to you to join a social circle, where you knew the great themes of evangelical Christianity would be the leading topics of the evening? I do not affirm these things; but if they are so, if your own conscienc eassents to the substantial accuracy of this representation, what an affecting view have we presented to us of your moral condition!

You aspire, we will suppose, to the character of a cultivated and refined person. You are eager in the pursuit of knowledge. You search for it in the depth of the ocean, and along the star-lit galleries of the firmament. You can spend hours in analyzing a flower or decomposing a drop of water. You are willing to take lessons from the birds, the fishes, the insects, from the very pebbles under you feet. You range through all history. You study foreign languages, that you may explore the libraries and decipher the monuments of other lands. Wherever knowledge is to be acquired, in the humblest repositories or in the most inaccessible, you are ready for the effort. But it is all with this single and most remarkable exception. Here is a volume which contains more truth, and truth of greater importance, than all other volumes combined. Where other books deal in guesses and hypotheses, and where nature is silent, this book speaks with distinctness, with fulness, and with authority. It is in fact the only source to which we can look for satisfactory information respecting our Creator, ourselves, and the way of salvation. And it is commended to us by having impressed upon it that sublime title, "THE WISDOM OF GOD." Yet from *this* book you turn away! The volume which, it might be presumed, would draw every lover of truth to its pages with an irresistible attraction, is the very work which you find jejune and prosaic; so much so, that it even imparts the same taint to every work deduced from it.

If the cause of this phenomenon be inquired into, it will readily be discovered. The Bible is not simply a book of science or a book of literature, but a religious book. We must eliminate the religious element, if we wish to invest it with the charms which belong to so many uninspired productions. Man thirsts for knowledge; *but even his desire of knowledge is not so strong as his enmity to God*, and he will sooner forego the indulgence of one of his most powerful natural appetites, than gratify it at the cost of being brought into immediate intercourse with his Maker. He will pursue truth with an unfaltering step, and an unslumbering eye throughout the universe, until she enters that refulgent sphere where the throne of God and of the Lamb is; then, as if smitten by a paralysis or struck with insanity, he can no longer discern any form or comeliness in her, and she has no beauty that he should desire her. The moment she arrays herself in the vestments of *holiness*, she becomes as much an object of repulsion as she had before been of loveliness. Clad in the coarsest fabrics of earth, she is sure of his homage; transfigured in the splendours of the uncreated glory, and his veneration is changed to hatred.

You will not say that this sketch is

unreal or exaggerated. It is vindicated by the confessions of too many individuals to be set aside as savouring of extravagance. The fact it assumes is one to be seriously pondered, viz.: the prevalence among so many, even educated persons, of a positive antipathy to religious truth; the utter distaste which you yourself may feel to the reading of the Bible and to serious reflection on its teachings. Nor is this the whole truth. Connect with the fact just stated, the feelings sometimes, perhaps habitually, awakened in your bosom when the claims of religion are pressed home upon you for immediate action. Are you not conscious on these occasions of a great repugnance to the subject? Are you not apt to feel that religion would interfere with your enjoyments? Do you not blend with it ideas of austerity and gloom, and treat it as you would some impending calamity which, since it could not be eluded altogether, you would avert as long as possible, and then submit to it with such resignation as you might command? And is it not under the influence of sentiments like these, that you so often put the subject away from you, and refuse even to *consider* it?

SECTION II.

ILLUSIVE PLEAS EXAMINED.

HERE, then, there is a palpable want of congruity between religion and your feelings. Is the fault with you or with religion? Is religion that harsh, cheerless, morose system which you have imagined it to be, or are your faculties so disordered that you have entirely mistaken its nature? For the sake of argument, let us assume that you are right in your estimate of religion. Let us suppose that it *is* a scheme of faith and morals adverse to present enjoyment; that it forbids even what we are accustomed to regard as innocent pleasures; that the life to which it calls us is a gloomy life; that its paths are full of thorns, with only here and there a flower, and that whatever it may promise for the future, it has little or nothing to recommend it in so far as this world is concerned.

Conceding all this, of what avail would it be in justifying or even extenuating your neglect of religion? The vital question is, whether Christianity is of God. If it is, all arguments drawn from its nature, with a view of discrediting its claims to our obedience, must be inconclusive and impertinent. For if Christianity is true, it proposes to us the only method of reconciliation to God, and the only means by which we can escape everlasting torments. What could be more idle, then, than to talk of the "inconveniences and trials" to which the reception of its doctrines might subject us? If a profession of Christianity even involved imminent personal peril; if, as in the early days of the church, we were liable to be hurried off from the Lord's Supper to the dungeon, or the stake,—what then? Is the rage of them who, at most, can only kill the body, to be more dreaded than His wrath who can destroy both soul and body in hell? Make the way to heaven as rough and thorny as you choose; multiply its obstacles; magnify its dangers; add any practicable amount of actual suffering, as the indispensable portion of every traveller,—so it really conducts to heaven, all these hinderances combined are not of the weight of a grain of sand, contemplated in their bearing upon the question, "What ought I to do?" The instant you concede the truth of the Bible, you are shut up to a foregone conclusion. It is at once the height of arrogance, and the extreme of folly, to admit that God has spoken to us, and then to palter about "considering and obeying" his commands, because the tone of them does not suit us, or obedience to them may expose us to trouble.

But we can stand upon firmer ground than this. The concession just made is a sheer gratuity. Religion is no such gloomy and prison-like system. Its mission in our world is one of God-like beneficence. Its hands are full of blessings. Its paths are peace. It confers substantial happiness here, as well as a title to perfect and eternal happiness hereafter. The evidences of this are within your reach. They are to be found in the Bible itself, and in the united testimony of all who have had experience of its benefits. Not indeed that a religious life involves no difficulties. It is justly represented as a warfare—an exterminating warfare. It must needs be a road somewhat rough and dangerous which leads from a revolted world to heaven. But the very fact that you can conceive of this system as one hostile to your present enjoyment, and adapted to throw the sombre hues of the grave over all that is bright and cheerful in life, illustrates the evil tendency of your inconsideration. You are repelled from the consideration of it because it wears to your eye so lowering an aspect. If you *must* barter away your cheerfulness, you will at least postpone the sacrifice as long as possible.

Do you not believe that God is a Being of infinite goodness and mercy, and that he delights, not in the misery, but in the happiness of his creatures? Does not this very scheme of religion, about which we are arguing, attest his concern for our welfare, in a manner adapted to silence all doubts and extinguish all skepticism? Is the sentiment to be tolerated for one moment, that he who so loved the world, as to give his only-begotten Son to die for it, could frame a system of religion, in any the least particular unfavourable to our well-being? Can you persuade yourself, that he who spared not his own Son, but delivered him up for us all, will not with him also freely give us all things?

Whence, then, these most unwarrantable suspicions about the proper effects of religion? Whence these injurious prejudices against it, as being adverse to rational and elevated happiness? If, as you admit, it bears God's image and superscription, how can you think of it as a sour and ascetic scheme, or suppose it would require of you any sacrifice which is not demanded by your own good? If you will but *reason* a little on the subject, you will find ample cause to distrust your impressions as to its nature, as you will certainly see both the injustice and the impolicy of being deterred by such a prejudice, from a careful consideration of its claims. Nay, if you are disposed to deal honestly with yourself, you will find material for sober reflection, in the very fact that religion should wear this forbidding guise; that adapted and intended, as your reason no less than revelation assures you it must be, to comfort and bless you, it should suggest to your minds only images of sadness or terror. How unavoidable the presumption, that you must be labouring under some gross hallucination; that some violent disease has impaired and confounded your faculties; that the defects you attribute to religion are in your own character; and that your repugnance to it is a startling proof, how much you stand in need of its healing power.

This neglect of it, however, is to be but temporary. You find a shelter from the reproaches of the Bible, and of your own conscience, in the reflection that by-and-by the subject *shall* be considered; that you will take it up, and make amends, by a thorough examination, for your present indifference to it. But why should you do this? Why not dismiss the subject altogether? If it is so unwelcome to you, why let it project its dark shadows athwart your future path, and obscure the serenity of your declining years? You are ready with your answer: — "It would be madness to banish finally a subject which involves my well-being for eternity. I must attend to it sooner or later, or be lost forever."

Will you do yourself the justice to weigh the import of this answer? You "*must* consider the subject of religion hereafter, because it involves your well-being for eternity." Give me leave to put this in another form, without altering the sense. "On my reception or rejection of the gospel offer, is suspended my everlasting destiny. If, through the mercy and grace of God, I embrace it, I shall at my death ascend to heaven, and be perfectly holy and happy forever. If I refuse or neglect to embrace it, I must, at death, be cast into outer darkness. Hell will be my home; the devils and lost spirits my companions; I must lie down in the unquenchable fire, and endure the gnawings of the worm that never dies. This doom may overtake me at any moment, since nothing is more precarious than life. *Therefore,* in order to escape so horrible a destiny, I must hereafter, at some undefined period, when my antipathy to religion shall have vanished, give attention to the subject, and make preparation for a change of worlds!" Such is the import of your language, without the slightest colouring. And in what light does it present your inconsideration? Did you ever hear of so impotent a conclusion, from such majestic premises? Were logic and reason ever before so put to shame? Were eternal things ever treated with such grave trifling? You will consider of religion hereafter, because if you die, (which you may do to-day,) without having attended to it, you are lost beyond redemption! And in this purpose you rest, simply from "the want of a disposition" to apply your mind to the subject now. You "feel no interest" in the matter at present, and you must wait until you do; when that auspicious day arrives, that you are disposed to hear what God has to say to you, you will listen to his communications!

Reference has already been made to the indignity which this conduct casts upon the Supreme Being. Not to revert to that topic here, do you not perceive, in the state of feeling in question, a most cogent argument why you should bring your mind into instant and earnest contact with the gospel? The greater your aversion to this, the more palpable your need of it. This aversion is the vital principle of the malady you are seized with, and for which the gospel is the only antidote. It stands forth, a convincing and solemn memento of that violent disjunction between your soul and God, which can be removed only through your sincere repentance and faith in the Redeemer. And when you talk of waiting until you feel sufficient "interest" in the matter to give heed to it, can you suppose that the course you are pursuing is adapted to bring about this desired change in your feelings? Will your love of the world be diminished, by a continued devotion to the world? Will the power of sin over you be abated by indulgence in sin? Will your wayward passions and attachments be weakened by gratification? "Are you so thoughtless or unknowing, as to fancy that a long course of estrangement from your higher interest, of aversion to it, of resistance against its claims, of suppression of the remonstrances of conscience in its behalf, is to leave you in a kind of mental state, impartial to admit at length the conviction, that now it is high time, and easily convertible into a Christian spirit? Consider that all this time you are forming the habits, which, when inveterately established, will either be invincibly upon you through life, or require a mighty wrench to emancipate you. This refusal to think; this revolting from any attempt at self-examination; this averting of your attention from serious books; this declining to seek the Divine favour and assistance by prayer; this projecting of schemes bearing no regard to that favour, and which are not to need that assistance; this eagerness to seize each transitory pleasure; this preference of companions, who, perhaps, would like you the worse, if they thought you feared God, or cared for your eternal welfare;—these dispositions, prolonged in a succession of your willing acquiescences in them, will grow into a settled constitution of your soul, which will thus become its own inexorable tyrant. The habit so forming will draw in to it all the affections, the workings of imagination, and the trains of thought; will so possess itself of them, that in it alone they will live, and move, and have their being. It will have a strong, unremitting propensity to grow entire, so as to leave nothing unpreoccupied in the mind, for any opposing agent to take hold on, in order to counteract it, as if it were instinctively apprehensive of the effect of protests from conscience, or visitings from the powers of heaven, or intimations from the realm of death; and, therefore, intent on forming the sentiments of the soul to such a consistence and coalition, as shall leave none of them free to desert at the voice of these summoners."*

It is, indeed, a monstrous deception you practise upon yourself, when you fancy that a course of implicit submission to these earth-born propensities will ultimately generate a disposition to break away from the bondage they impose. As well might the inebriate pretend that prolonged indulgence in his cups would by-and-by evolve a disgust for the poison which is consuming him; or the husbandman, that a thorough

* Foster.

seeding his plantation with thistles, would guarantee a generous harvest of grain. It is a strange way of insuring the renovation of your character, to foster principles and habits which are in flagrant antagonism to all holiness. These very habits and principles constitute the grand hinderance to your salvation now; they operate with such potency as even to inspire an antipathy to all reflection on your spiritual state. By what alchemy are they to be transmuted into monitors to repentance and stimulants to a holy life? How is an ever-increasing alienation from God to facilitate your return to him? If you have no inclination to return now, why should you have when the distance which separates you from him has been indefinitely increased?

The conclusions to which so many lines of abstract argument conduct us, may be tested by observation and experience. You will be able, without going beyond the sphere of your daily walks, to find individuals who have long occupied the ground you stand upon. Twenty, thirty, forty years ago, when pressed with the obligation of immediate repentance, they resisted and deferred it on the ground that they then "felt no disposition" to consider it. They had the full purpose of complying with it, but deemed it advisable to wait until their indifference had passed away. Has it passed away, or are they waiting still? To your eyes, however it may be to their own, the case is too plain and too affecting to need an interpreter. You see how, during all this period, they have been heaping up obstacles between themselves and heaven. By a silent and gradual process, they have invigorated their secular principles, and become more completely saturated with the spirit of the world. The net-work of earthly passions and projects which encloses them, once so fragile, is intricate and compact. Avenues to their consciences, which were once open, are shut up. They are less sensitive to the appeals of Scripture. It is more difficult to arouse them to wholesome meditation upon their prospects for eternity. They have the same latent intention of repentance; but when you look at the superincumbent mass of earthliness and sin which has accumulated upon it, you feel that nothing short of a miracle can ever vitalize it, so as to convert the purpose to repent into actual repentance.

All this is as clear as the meridian sun to your eyes, in respect to many persons whom you have seen growing old or approximating to old age in the neglect of religion. And is there not something still nearer home to corroborate it? Can you not refer to a period *in your own experience,* when the ascendency of the world over you was less complete than it is now? Has the result justified your calculation, that the lapse of time would abate your disinclination to serious thought? Is your repugnance to prayer and to the study of the Scriptures diminished? Do you find it more difficult to ward off the shafts of divine truth, as they reach you in the sanctuary? Have you a keener sense of the vanity of earth, and a growing disposition to engage in the service of God? Or is the reverse of all this true? Is the tide of worldliness rising higher and higher, and gradually filling up every interstice of your heart? Has the broad current of your thoughts and affections become thoroughly impregnated with a mere earthly spirit? Are you living for this world alone? Are your avocations, your plans, your pleasures, your hopes, your associations, absorbed with the things which are seen and temporal, to the exclusion of the things which are unseen and eternal? And when, in some better moment, a stroke of Providence, a sermon, or some other agency happens to disturb your spiritual torpor, and awaken a feeling of remorse and uneasiness, do you find it a lighter task than it once was to smother these self-reproaches and resume your wonted levity? Surely, then, you can interpret these omens also. You require no prophet from heaven to assure you that they bear the same evil significancy with the kindred portents you so readily decipher in the case of your friends and neighbours. They are the handwriting on the wall over-against you; and they admonish you, in no ambiguous symbols, of impending destruction, if you go on trusting to a life of worldliness to extinguish your repugnance to the gospel.

There is also implied, in this inconsideration, a very inadequate conception of the work we have to do, and of the time demanded to do it properly. We find in the Bible expressions like these: "Strive to enter in at the strait gate." "Giving all diligence, make your calling and election sure." "He that endureth to the end shall be saved." "If the righteous scarcely be saved, where shall the ungodly and the sinner appear?" Salvation, then, is a difficult work. It is a great thing to be a Christian. Colossal obstructions bar the way to heaven. Every step has its dangers.

> "'Tis but a few that find the gate,
> While crowds mistake and die."

Could we see things as they are,—the deliverance of a soul from spiritual death, its liberation from the bondage of Satan, its enfranchisement with the rights and privileges of Christ's kingdom, its gradual transformation into the divine image, its triumph over all its enemies, and its final entrance into the realms of glory, we should be no less awe-struck with the difficulty and grandeur of this achievement, than filled with admiration at the boundless wisdom, power, and grace displayed in accomplishing it. Marathon and Thermopylæ, Trafalgar and Waterloo, the proudest of earth's battle-fields, wheresoever they may be found, dwindle into insignificance when compared with the mighty conflict involved in the *salvation* of a single individual. Yet this sublime and most arduous undertaking, *you* would thrust into a mere corner of human life. Instead of making every thing give way to it, you allow every thing to take precedence of it. You make it wait on business, on study, on pleasure, on social engagements, on indolence, on indifference. There is absolutely nothing in life, however insignificant and contemptible, that this vast interest, which comprehends eternity in its issue, is not, with one person or another, compelled to wait on it. Life were short enough to do it justice, had you taken it up with the dawn of your moral agency and prosecuted it until you fell asleep in death. But it has been pushed along, year after year,—the difficulty of the work increasing as the space for performing it has been diminished,—until to-day *you have more work to do and less time to do it in, than you ever had before.* Nay, you are possibly even now parleying with yourself whether you shall not postpone its claims still longer. Does it at all occur to you what these questions are, which you adjourn with so fatal a facility to all the trivialities of the passing moment, which you even dismiss because you happen not to be *in a mood* to consider them? Alas! it is this very inconsideration which betrays you into the infatuated course we are deploring. It is not that you do not know, but because you do not consider that it is your own SALVATION which is at stake. It is the question, "How may I escape from hell and fly to heaven?" that you are forcing into some little parenthesis of your little future,—handing it over, peradventure, to the puerilities of a miserable dotage, or to the weakness, the sufferings, and the dismay of an unexpected death-bed. And wherefore? Is there any invincible necessity laid upon you to submit to this strange mal-adjustment of your concerns, this transfer of the very greatest and most momentous of your affairs, to the very worst season in your whole life for attending to them? No, you might just as well—yea, ten thousand times better—provide for these interests sooner. But you must needs use the vigour of your faculties and the flower of your time for other ends. This world is to be looked after. First the body, then the soul. Time first, eternity afterward. Thus the soul is robbed and ruined. What ought to be the prime business of life is delayed till the spark of life is about going out. What ought to engross all the powers of mind and body throughout the entire limit of our mortal probation, is assigned to the hapless decrepitude of old age. With the ocean of eternity before you, instead of employing the time God has given you in making preparation for your endless voyage, you waste it upon comparative trifles, and leave your whole preparation to the moment when you may be summoned to embark! This is not the design, but this is, in every instance of delay, the possible, as it is in innumerable instances the actual, result. To neglect to prepare to-day, abridges by so much your time and opportunity for preparing, and may preclude it altogether.

You will not admit this. You have no thought of going into eternity unprepared. You almost resent the suggestion that you may be so infatuated as to reserve for it only the closing days or hours of life. But if this is not your purpose, what is? If you are resolved not to remit the serious consideration of religion to a death-bed, *when* is it to be taken up? Is the day marked in your diary? Is the purpose drawn up and put on file with the plans you have framed respecting your worldly affairs? If you were pressed to answer these questions, would not the humiliating confession be extorted from you, that this is a matter about which you have *no* plan; that while every possible arrangement is made concerning your earthly interests, you have fixed upon no period for looking after your immortal interests; that you have, in fact, simply a general purpose of making your peace with God; but whether it is to be undertaken on this day twelvemonth, or this day ten years, or at any other specific date, is a point you have not settled.

Now, on this admission, it is no injustice to you to allege that you *are* virtually remitting this great interest to your death-bed. A merciful God may interpose and prevent this procrastination; but, in so far as you are concerned, there is every probability that it will be delayed until the prospect of a speedy dissolution forces it upon your attention. There are thousands of individuals every year who are brought to this result by the identical process through which you are passing. Relying through life on a vague and delusive purpose of embracing the gospel offer "at some period," they are astonished, at length, (they need not have been, for it was precisely what they might have expected,) to find themselves grappling with death without out any equipment for the encounter. Often are individuals of this kind heard bemoaning their folly and criminality, waking up to the consciousness that it is a sad time to prepare for eternity, when the blood is chilling in the arteries, and the affrighted soul is waiting, trembling and agonized, for the walls of its clay tenement to fall and leave it houseless, portionless, hopeless, under the piercing gaze of an injured and avenging God! And why may it not be so with *you?* You are treading the same path they trod. You are trusting to the same visionary hopes. You are vindicating or excusing your inconsideration by the same gossamer-like apologies. Like you, they "felt no interest" in religion, and had too little energy to bring themselves to the examination of it. Like you, they were resolved to attend to it long before death should summon them away. Like you, they permitted one earthly object and pursuit after another to beguile their time and steal away their affections. Like you, they grew insensibly hardened by this course of worldliness and this habitual resistance to divine truth. And will it be surprising, if, having thus cast in your lot with them through so large a part of the way, you should go on with them to the close, and have your dying moments harassed with the gloom and the consternation which marked their passage into eternity?

But why argue this point? Every

thing is conceded, when you admit, what no one has the presumption to deny, that death may come for you at any moment; that your winding-sheet may even now be in the fuller's hands; and the shaft on its unerring flight, which is to transfix your heart. This fact alone might suffice to show you, that, in neglecting to consider the claims of religion, you are putting your everlasting all in jeopardy; that a single day's delay may involve an eternity of unavailing remorse and sorrow.

Here then let me pause long enough to inquire whether it is possible for you, even to extenuate the guilt and folly of this inconsideration, by any of those pleas or pretexts which have hitherto satisfied you. Remember that when God charges this neglect upon you as a sin, it is your own happiness, no less than his sovereignty, which is implicated in the allegation. The crime you are guilty of is a crime against your own rational and immortal nature. You ought to be happy. You might be happy. God requires you to be happy; and has placed the means within your reach, at an infinite cost to himself, though as free as the air of heaven to you. Yet you decline his bounty. You even refuse to "consider" the sublime and glorious scheme through which he proposes it to you. And the barrier behind which you shelter yourself when this conduct is brought home to you as a sin, is that "your feelings are not interested in the matter," and therefore you cannot attend to it. Why should they be interested unless you have tried to have them so? Suppose you deal with this subject as you would deal with a question of commerce or a question of history, with a branch of science or a personal accomplishment. Bring your mind to the patient study of the Bible. Commune with your own heart. Call upon God in prayer. Rouse yourself from your lethargy. Feel that religion is a reality; and that your soul is to be saved through the blood of the cross, or to perish eternally. Do this and see whether you cannot surmount this fearful torpor which threatens to destroy you forever.

SECTION III.

THE PRETEXTS FOR NEGLECTING RELIGION IRRATIONAL AND SORDID.

I HAVE shown, that where there is an habitual indisposition to consider the claims of religion, that duty is likely to be remitted to a death-bed. It is proper, in this connection, to call your attention to the specific feeling which usually prompts to this delay. That feeling is, that there is no actual necessity, on the score of *personal safety*, for 'becoming religious' just now, and therefore it may be postponed for the present without hazard. If this course involved manifest and palpable danger, you would overcome your reluctance, and sit down to the careful examination of the subject. But as you see no danger, a little delay cannot be an evil of much moment.

Here, then, the whole question, whether religion shall receive your instant attention, is made to hinge on the point, whether it will put you in jeopardy to refuse. The demand which religion makes of you is, that you cease to do evil, and learn to do well; that you repent of your sins, and render to your Creator and Preserver that homage and obedience which are his due; that you trust in the Lord Jesus Christ for pardon, and walk henceforward in the way of his commands. It exacts of you no sacrifice; lays upon you no service; appoints you to no trial, which is not for your own good. It proffers you the protection and friendship of God, all needful succours and consolations in this world, and everlasting felicity and glory hereafter. These are the proposals religion makes to you; and it is in pondering such proposals, and to guide you in your disposition of them, that you raise the question, "Can I reject them for a time, without putting myself *in peril?* or, does my *safety* require me to accept them now?" You cannot fail, on a moment's reflection, to be struck with the utter want here indicated, of any due appreciation of the blessings tendered you, or any perception of the relations subsisting between the parties to this transaction. It might be supposed, with our instinctive and irrepressible desire of happiness, that blessings like these would be eagerly seized the moment they were placed within our reach; that the mere possibility of securing them would make any individual of our race willing to put forth the most unwearied exertions, and to submit to the greatest hardships. But, instead of this, we have the extraordinary spectacle presented to us, (nay, we all in turn present this spectacle,) of rebels consulting whether they can, with *prudence*, defer acceding to an offer of clemency from their Sovereign; of lost sinners, calculating how long it will be *safe* for them to go on in sin, before consenting to a free tender of salvation! In all this procrastination and paltering, the authority and rights of Jehovah are ignored; duty is set at defiance; the claims of reverence and gratitude are trampled in the dust; nothing is thought of, but the personal immunity of the transgressor. As long as he can do *without God*, he will; when dangers thicken, and death impends, he will seek his aid.

To say that the principle of action here assumed would excite universal abhorrence if carried into any department of secular or social life, is only to give utterance to a sentiment in which every generous mind must acquiesce. What reason is there, what fitness, in suspending our loyalty to God on his toleration of our sins; in resolving to disobey him, just so long as we fancy he will restrain his vengeance, and not cut us down in our impiety? No honourable man would deal thus with his neighbour, or with the government under which he lives. Does it sanctify a sordid principle that we have adopted it, not in our intercourse with our fellow-creatures, but in our conduct toward God? Are the same actions mercenary, when they have respect to a creature; and innocent, not to say commendable, when they terminate on the Creator?

The more this is pondered, the more clearly will it be seen, that in the scheme of life we are considering, the one element of *personal safety* is made to subserve the most unwarrantable and unworthy purposes.

It might be opportune to remark, that it is no less blind than perverse; that in seeking its own ends by its own means, it too commonly plucks down upon itself the ruin it would elude; and that true safety is to be found in doing God's will, not in resisting it. But waiving that topic, why surrender one's self to the control of this grovelling sentiment, as though, in our relations to the Deity, there were no room for any other? "Not knowing," says the apostle, "that *the goodness* of God leadeth thee to repentance."

Look around you at the tokens of His goodness. See how he has blessed you in your basket and in your store, in your health, in your business, in your family, in your country, in your manifold religious privileges. Review your life, and see how he has watched over you from childhood to this hour, with paternal affection; how often he has interposed to rescue you from difficulty or danger; and in how many forms he has carried forward his beneficent ministrations toward you. Is there no susceptibility in your breast, to which kindness like this appeals; no chord there which vibrates when these mercies pass in review before you? And when to these blessings you superadd the infinitely higher blessings of redemption, purchased with "blood divine," are you still unmoved? Can nothing stir that leaden torpor, that Dead Sea stagnation, within, but the sense of impending wrath? Has gratitude no place there? Shall your bosom thrill with thankfulness whenever you receive the most trivial kindness from a fellow-creature, and be unimpressed by all the affluence of that bounty which Jehovah is lavishing upon you? You will not say that this is right.

You will admit that it is all wrong. If you have the least spark of magnanimity, the slightest leaven of honourable and manly feeling, you will be abashed when you reflect on the principle which governs you in your intercourse with a Benefactor to whom you owe such infinite obligations.

In recording, some time since, the

decease of a very distinguished statesman, the newspapers stated that he was much occupied during his illness with the subject of religion; that he conversed often with the ministers of the gospel; avowed his cordial reception of the Christian faith, and in this state of mind passed into eternity. The narrative was in terms which implied that his preparation for death had been postponed until he was taken sick; and, indeed, it was well known, that however correct he might have been in his general deportment, he had never up to that time manifested any personal interest in religion. In all this, he was the representative of a very numerous body of persons; for similar examples are constantly occurring in every walk of life.

Now, in looking at a scene like this, every one must commend this solicitude about the soul, even though it has been so long delayed. Far better to repent with the dying malefactor than not to repent at all. Better to strive to enter in at the strait gate at the eleventh hour,—yes, better even to strive and fail, than to die in utter unconcern and stupidity. But contemplate this spectacle in another aspect. Here is a man (the case occurs daily) forty, fifty, possibly sixty years of age. He has spent his life in the bosom of a Christian community. Every day has come to him freighted with blessings. He has always had the Bible within his reach. He has weekly heard, or might have heard, the preaching of the gospel. God has called him to repentance in innumerable ways. His duty has been set before him in the clearest manner. He has been reasoned with, warned, exhorted, entreated to make his peace with God, and to give his influence to religion. But he has steadily refused. He has, possibly, been unwilling even to *consider* the claims of God upon him. Absorbed with other things, carried away by the lust of the flesh, the lust of the eyes, and the pride of life, he has sought his own ends, lived only for the world, and left Christianity to fight its own battles, careless whether they terminated in victory or defeat. Disease lays its iron grasp upon this proud votary of the world, and conducts him into that chamber from which he is never to come forth until his remains are carried to their last resting-place. Assured by his physicians (and not till then) of the serious nature of his malady, he begins to consider his ways. He calls for the Bible; so long neglected that he knows not where to read. He procures other religious books, which may aid him in getting clearer views of the way of life. He sends for a Christian friend or pastor to counsel him, and tell him what he must do to be saved. He is frequent and earnest in his supplications for the Divine mercy. And thus he is hastening his preparation for a change of worlds. In all this, he is acting wisely. But what a miserable return is he making to God! His health, time, talents, property, influence, all have been expended upon selfish and earthly objects; and now that he *dare* not and *cannot* cleave to these any longer, he will turn to God! No love to God prompts him, no gratitude, no ingenuous sentiment of contrition, no dissatisfaction with the world: if he could with safety, he would cling to his idol still. Death is at the door: this is the sole secret of his anxiety. He comes to dedicate to his Maker his shattered powers, and the few hours that may remain to him, simply because, if he neglects this, a terrible retribution will presently overtake him.

You see, as distinctly as I can, the true tenor of this transaction. But "it is not to be thus with you." You have too much elevation of character to think of putting the Deity off with so paltry an offering. You are not ready to consider the subject of religion now, but you fully purpose to do it before you are prostrated with a mortal disease.

Without impugning the sincerity of this intention, it may be allowed me to ask, whether the principle it proceeds upon is essentially better than the one exemplified in the case just considered.

It is the prayer of Augustine over again: "Lord, convert me; but not yet!" It recognises the obligation to serve him, but practically denies his claim to your whole time, and your entire influence. It assumes that your first duty is to the world; and that it will be enough if you devote yourself to God after you shall, for an indefinite period, have lived for the world. You cannot be ignorant, that where this ground is taken, the common result is substantially the same as in the example already noted: the lion's share goes to the world,—the meager remnant, if any, to God. It is, in any event, a deliberate determination to abridge your means and opportunities of doing his will and promoting his glory.

Can this be justified? Can it be extenuated? Is life, fleeting, evanescent life, too long a period to be employed in serving the Being who bestowed life upon you? Would your undivided homage be too opulent a return for the favours you have received from him? Is it the acknowledgment which your own reason and conscience assure you is befitting the relations you sustain to him, to exhaust the vigour of your faculties in the prosecution of mere earthly objects, and appropriate to him only your days of decline and inactivity, if not of decrepitude? Conceding that you may live to old age, and that death will then await your plenary preparation for his summons; how much more honourable would it be to come now, and lay your thrift and enterprise, your genial affections and noble aspirations upon his altar, than to put Him off with the impoverished refuse of a life of sin and folly!

Besides, how erroneous and unworthy a *conception of religion* is that involved in this and its affiliated schemes of life! In a company of military officers, (one of whom was a personal friend of the writer's,) the question one day came up, whether it was expedient to permit clergymen to visit the sick. Not to recite the other opinions, "My notion," said the surgeon of the corps, "is, that such visits are proper in certain circumstances. When the physician has done all he can for a man, and gives him up, then, I think, it is proper to send for the clergyman." You will smile at the ignorance and irrationality displayed in this remark; but it is not very much aside from the popular idea of religion. If you will analyze the schemes which you are cherishing, you will probably find that religion is contemplated rather as a provision for death than a chart of life; much more as a bridge, over which we are to pass into heaven, than as a highway, along which we are to travel through this world. The feeling is, "I cannot die without religion, but I can live without it." And so you think it very well for the infirm, and the aged, and invalids of every sort to become religious; but there is no reason why the hearty and vigorous, who are engaged in active duties, should be in haste about it. In other words, there is no reason why you should not sacrifice all the sound and the fat of your flock to mammon, and put God off with the lame, and the blind, and the sick. There is no reason why you should not expend the energies of your being upon yourselves, and dedicate your withered faculties to your Creator.

THIS IS NOT CHRISTIANITY. Religion, it is true, is rich in its consolations, and supplies our only adequate support in sickness and trouble. But it is no less a scheme of duty than a means of comfort. It was merely nor mainly to provide comfort for his people that Christ died, but to make them holy; not simply that they might get to heaven themselves, but that they might help others in getting there also. He challenges our undivided allegiance. He insists upon the subjugation of all our powers and passions to his will; upon the thorough extirpation of our sinful principles and habits, and the gradual moulding of our whole characters into his image. He demands that we serve him in our several stations and relations; that we be governed by the Scripture code of morals; that we subordinate every earthly pursuit to his glory, and the welfare of his kingdom; and that, in our respective spheres, we do our best to maintain the character implied in those expressive emblems, "Ye are the light of the world;" "Ye are the salt of the earth." Our own good requires this. The present life is the vestibule to eternity. We are here to be trained for a higher stage of being. It is a great achievement to prepare a race so depraved for so lofty a destiny. It must needs be (unless God should choose to work a miracle) a tedious and painful process to fit such creatures as we are for citezenship in the New Jerusalem. It is a process which may well fill up the brief span of human life, and which it were gross infatuation to postpone to any other interest whatever.

Religion comprehends this wise and needful tutelage. It exerts its prerogative over the entire range of human life, from the cradle to the grave; from the most subtle purpose that lurks in the innermost chambers of the heart, to the sublimest transactions of cabinets and empires. It is impossible to escape from its authority, even for a moment. It never intermits its claims upon us. It stoops to no compromises with the world. It ceases not to cry in our ears, "Thou shalt love the Lord thy God with ALL thy heart, and thy neighbour as thyself."

Could it do less? Would it be a religion worthy of God, or suited to man, if it did not thus enjoin upon every child of Adam supreme and constant loyalty to Jehovah? On what ground, then, would you delay a compliance with its requisitions? If it is reasonable that God should require your whole time, if your own good also demands it, why voluntarily shorten the period you can devote to him, and lose the advantages to be derived from the culture of the Christian graces? It is surely an ungenerous temper which would put you upon grasping after the rewards of Christ's kingdom, without rendering him the stipulated service; which would make you eager for the crown, but unwilling to bear the cross. Had he dealt with us on this principle, the cross had never been set up, and we had all gone down to irretrievable and eternal ruin.

And why, (to glance at another phase of the selfishness on which we are commenting,) why should you not do your part in carrying forward the great and glorious work of human amelioration?

Look over the world, and see how full it is of sin, and suffering, and sorrow. Open your eyes upon the very neighbourhood in which you dwell, and see whether there be not at your very door a broad field for the exercise of Christian philanthropy. Survey our beloved country, and watch the torrents of infidelity and vice that are deluging the land. Whose office is it to counterwork these pestiferous agencies? Who is to explore these habitations of penury and ignorance; to gather the young into Sabbath-schools and day-schools; to visit the prisoners; to reclaim the intemperate, to circulate the Scriptures; to promote the due observance of the Sabbath; to send missionaries to every destitute spot, and to aid the Church in sustaining her benevolent institutions? Is there any obligation resting upon others to do this, which does not rest on you? It will not do for any of us to ask, "Am I my brother's keeper?" Linked together by the ties of a common humanity, we are responsible for the influence we exert upon each other's characters and destiny. No man may lawfully attempt to isolate himself from his race, and seek only his own interest. God will hold us accountable for the good we might have done, and have refused or neglected to do. Christianity needs your help in carrying forward her schemes of relief. There are forces enough arrayed against her without your opposition or indifference. Christ demands your co-operation with his people, in making his atonement known to all your fellow-creatures, and placing the means of grace within their reach. The service to which he calls you is a most reasonable service. His right to demand it is perfect. It is more worthy of your powers than any thing else in which you can engage. Is there any, even plausible ground on which you can refuse your aid in promoting the temporal happiness and the eternal salvation of our ruined race? Would it be generous even if you could do it without sin and without imperiling your own soul, to devolve all this work upon others; to shut your ears against the voice of Christ himself, through whom you hope yet to be saved, when he says to you, "Go work for me in doing good to your fellow-sinners; and whatsoever you do to the least of them for my sake, I will regard it as if done to me!"

Consider, further, that in assigning to the service of religion only some vague and precarious portion of your future life, (which may prove to be no portion of it at all,) the intermediate period, whether longer or shorter, is not to be a mere blank, without influence upon your character and upon your ultimate prospects of salvation. You are disinclined to take up the subject of religion now, because you "feel no interest" in it. I have already shown you the fallacy of supposing, that the continued neglect of religion can generate a disposition to "consider" it.

But note further, that during this undefined period which is still to precede your anticipated repentance, you are to be drinking in the spirit of worldliness, and travelling to a still greater distance from God. It seems strangely incongruous to talk of "repentance" in this connection. "Repentance" for what? Suppose death should not step in and extinguish your hopes in the blackness of an eternal night; suppose you reach the point, the distant, shadowy, receding point, where you are to be sated with the world and ready to abandon it, *what do you propose to repent of?* If you refer to the sins of your past lives, it seems quite reasonable. There are enough of them to call for bitter tears and the deepest humiliation. It is a fearful sight to look back over a whole life, and see nothing there but sin. There is a call for repentance. But your plan comprises more than this. You mean to repent of other sins; *sins not yet committed.* You mean to repent of the course you are just now entering upon. You form a purpose to-day not to consider the subject of religion now, with the avowed intention of mourning over that purpose hereafter! You decline a gracious call of the gospel, with the distinct avowal that you mean to lament that you declined it, and to ask God's forgiveness! You set out upon a path which you declare your intention to retrace, every step of it, with tears! This *is* mysterious. Were you to banish the subject altogether, and brave the consequences of going into eternity without repentance or faith in Christ, you might at least claim the merit of consistency. But this idea of sinning only that you may repent; of laughing to-day, that you may weep over your mirth to-morrow; of heaping up obstacles between your soul and heaven, that you may by-and-by remove them with a sorrowful heart; of pressing on toward the very verge of the bottomless pit, that you may at length, when the earth begins to cave from under your feet, fly back affrighted at your temerity, and seek the refuge you now scorn,—what name can be given to a career like this! And if the actors in it were other parties, and you the spectators, what alternative would you feel forced upon you in seeking a solution of the strange phenomenon, but that they were either bereft of reason, or under the sway of a hostility to God and his service, so inveterate as to be proof against all human agencies?

If these plain allegations have not offended you, you may possibly assent to their substantial verity. You may be ready to go as far as the Bible itself in condemning the unreasonableness and the criminality of your inconsideration; yet you may say, the *fact* of your indifference remains. You "do not feel sufficient interest in the matter" to take it up, and you have no resource but to defer it till you do; and as this is (so you imagine) "a thing beyond your own control," you are the more disposed to let it rest for the present.

I have throughout this whole discussion recognised the reality of this difficulty. Foolish as it is, criminal as it is, dangerous as it is, this "lack of interest" in religion constitutes a real and formidable hinderance in the way of a proper examination of the subject. But as no one will presume to plead it at the last day as an excuse for his impenitence, so we must beware how we treat it with a mistaken leniency now. The very consciousness of this aversion to serious things ought to alarm you. It is the white spot upon the surface which indicates the leprosy within, and to neglect the symptom is to trifle with the disease. The feeling, too, that this indifference is absolutely beyond your control, is but another effect of your insidious malady. It is true you cannot change your own heart, nor can you by a mere volition replace your spiritual apathy, with that solicitude about the concerns of eternity which you persuade yourself you would *like* to experience.

But there are certain other things which are within the compass of your own volitions. If you are not practising self-dissimulation, if you sincerely desire to "become interested in religion," you will leave no practicable means untried to bring about so important an end. What, then, can you do? You can determine, in dependence on the help of God, to enter upon the careful and thorough examination of the subject. You can deal with it as you would with any literary, political, or professional question which might require your attention. As a physician, you might have to grapple with some disease you had never heard of. As a lawyer, you might find it necessary to investigate a case which was extremely distasteful to you. As a merchant, the course of trade might force you into laborious researches in some department of commerce which you had always shrunk from with aversion. But in these exigencies, your policy would be decisive and onward. You could not respect yourself, if you sat down quietly and succumbed to your feeling of indifference. Gathering up your mental energies, you would assail the obnoxious topic with a vigorous determination to master it. You would make it the theme of your studies and reflections, and avail yourself of all the light that could be brought to bear upon it. And according to the established course of things, your antipathy would give way and your interest would increase as you prosecuted your inquest.

What has CHRISTIANITY done, that it is not entitled to the same treatment at your hands? Why should you not extend to it the fair and manly dealing you mete out to any and every secular matter in which you are implicated? It is just as competent to you to employ your powers in examining a question of theology as a question of jurisprudence or a question of merchandise. You can as well set about the systematic reading of the BIBLE, as the systematic study of history, metaphysics, or any other branch of literature. You can take up some sterling religious book, like Hodge's Way of Life, Wilberforce's Practical View, Gregory's Letters, Scott's Force of Truth, or Alexander's Religious Experience, and appropriate a specific part of every twenty-four hours to the private and thoughtful perusal of it. You can read with a constant reference to your own character. You can accompany the exercise with fervent prayer for divine assistance. You can be earnest in invoking the Holy Spirit to deliver you from error and unbelief, to subdue your evil passions, to remove your indifference, to convince you of sin, and to lead you to Christ. You can avoid, in a measure, those scenes and associations, and put away those habits, which are unfavourable to serious reflection. You can converse with your pastor, and frequent the sanctuary, and attend the weekly religious services of the congregation to which you belong, and seek the society of Christian people, and court such influences as are adapted to foster your good purposes and enliven your apprehension of "the powers and terrors" of the world to come. When you have finished one book, you can read another and another. You can do all this with the feeling that religion is no longer to be tampered with; that your soul is too precious to be enticed to hell by the visionary purpose of *future* repentance; that, however it may be with others, the time has come for *you* to make your peace with God; and that, God helping you, nothing shall divert you from this work, until you are washed from your sins in the blood of the cross, and made a new creature in Christ Jesus.

These things you can do. These things you ought to do. And should you do them—with humility, with perseverance, with importunate prayer—can you doubt as to the result? Do you not believe that your indifference would soon vanish? that what you had undertaken from a sheer conviction of duty, would presently awaken the dormant sensibilities of your soul; that what was at first a matter of pure intellect, would become no less a matter of feeling; that religion would begin to unfold itself to your mind in the solemn grandeur of its proportions, as at once the most august and the most urgent of all interests; and that, from being a mere denizen of earth, living only for the world, without a thought, perhaps, of God and eternity, you would find yourself engrossed with the one question, "WHAT MUST I DO TO BE SAVED?" and pressing into the kingdom of heaven with an energy that would brook no delay? Can you doubt that something like this would follow? And if you believe it would, *can you refuse to make the trial?*

SECTION IV.

ENCOURAGEMENTS.

Up to this point it has been my aim to exhibit the true nature, and counteract the influence of that "lack of interest" in the subject of religion, which has made you unwilling to sit down to the serious consideration of it. If I have at all succeeded in dispelling the sophistries and self-illusions which usually pertain to this state of mind, and in showing that this indifference to religion is a matter very much within your own control, there is one specious suggestion which may still ensnare you. You may hesitate about entering upon the course of reading and reflection proposed to you, from a feeling of distrust as to the ultimate result. There are "difficulties" in the way, and you are "not *certain*" that you could surmount them. You "might set out and fail." Such is your conviction of the reasonableness and importance of the duty enjoined upon you, that nothing could deter you from giving your attention to the subject, if you believed it would "avail;" but having no assurance on this point, you shrink from undertaking it.

Here, again, the reality of the hinderance must be admitted. In all enterprises, hopefulness is one of the main elements of success. It is a sad drudgery to toil and fag at an occupation which promises to reward us only with disappointment. Where we have no encouragement, we have no resolution.

Without the prospect of attaining an end, we can have no heart to pursue it. And as this principle applies equally to spiritual and to temporal objects, it is not surprising that persons should hesitate about addressing themselves to the matter of their personal salvation, if they see no likelihood of securing it.

But, on the other hand, religion has cause to complain that it is not placed, as regards this point, on a footing with secular affairs. No politician insists upon certainty of success, before aspiring to a post of honour in the state. No physician refuses to cope with a disease until he is certain he can master it. The multifarious operations of commerce are all based upon contingent calculations. Individuals frequently expend a fortune in experimental mining or manufacturing, where, in the judgment of impartial observers, the probabilities of success are scarcely more than five in a hundred. And enlightened governments will lay out millions of money, and jeopard whole fleets, in exploring regions which are utterly inaccessible to commerce, and which, the more they are traversed, stamp with greater hopelessness the idea of turning them to any valuable practical use. Why not proceed in the same way in spiritual things? With what propriety can we demand a measure of certainty, in seeking our salvation, which we should pronounce very unreasonable in seeking fame or fortune? Why be disheartened, where the soul is concerned, with obstacles which would only sharpen the appetite and stimulate ambition, if it were a question of property, or a question of science? One might suppose that the whole bias of men's minds would be the other way; that the bare possibility of salvation would be sufficient to arouse them to the highest degree of effort; and that, instead of being retarded or repelled by difficulties, every new hinderance would be but a fresh incentive to exertion. Where life is concerned, this is the case. No man gives over caring for his health because his symptoms are unfavourable, or the remedial agents he wishes to employ difficult of access. "All that a man hath will he give for his life." The universal principle with invalids is, while there is life there is hope, and while there is hope, no means of cure must be neglected. How extraordinary, then, is it, that men should be so easily turned aside, where, instead of life, it is the SOUL which is at stake! But without stopping to speculate on the causes of a phenomenon which is, unhappily, so familiar that it has ceased to excite wonder, it is more to our present purpose to observe, that *there is actually less reason for discouragement in this, the most urgent and momentous of all pursuits, than there is in our common secular avocations.* Whatever grounds we may have for anticipating success in any financial or professional undertaking, we have more for expecting it in proper exertions to escape from the thraldom of sin. I say "proper exertions," because, in many cases, the effort is really not made in good faith; it is a mere languid, temporary striving, with which the heart has very little to do; and which must fail as a matter of course. But there is seldom any failure, where this object is pursued with the earnestness which men usually bring to the prosecution of their worldly schemes.

There is, however, a peculiarity about the search after religion, which ought to be noticed in this connection. Most persons have but vague ideas of what it is to "become religious." The entrance upon a Christian life is, to their minds, shrouded in mystery. They know that except they are "born again," they cannot see the kingdom of God, and that this change must be wrought by the Holy Spirit. The acknowledged greatness of the transformation, combined, perhaps, with the inspired account of the effusion of the Spirit on the day of Pentecost, has impressed them with the feeling, that if they are ever renewed, the Divine influence which is to effect it will come, "like a rushing, mighty wind," or in some other palpable manner, and *impel* them into the kingdom of heaven. They suppose that the operations of the Spirit upon the heart can ordinarily be distinguished from our own mental exercises; and that until we are *conscious* of his presence, it must be useless to set about the work of repentance. That a regenerated person may have a perfect assurance that the mighty transformation he has experienced was as much beyond the compass of his own powers as it would be to create a world, is an undoubted fact. But it is from the *Bible* we learn to ascribe every thing good in our exercises to the influence of the Spirit. He exerts his power upon us in a manner strictly adapted to the laws of our rational nature. "It is God which worketh in you both to will and to do of his good pleasure." Not only "to do," but even "to will." He touches and controls the secret springs of volition; so that when we "will," or determine to cease from sinning, to study the Scriptures, or to do any thing else which he has commanded, the impulse and the strength really come from the Spirit. We are *conscious* of the determination or choice, (with the motives which induce it,) and in this, of course, we are perfectly voluntary. But there is a mysterious power at work back of our volitions, and secretly prompting them. And it is on this very ground the apostle bids us "work out our own salvation." See Phil. ii. 12, 13. The Spirit is waking us from our slumber; therefore, we should yield to the bias he is giving to our inclinations, and put forth our earnest efforts in the same direction. To expect that he will disclose his agency to our minds, is to mistake the whole character of his functions. Our Saviour compares his influence to the wind, which is invisible, silent, and penetrating. You are waiting, you say, for the Spirit to come and change your heart. Has not the Spirit visited you already? Are you not thoughtful about your soul's concerns? Do you not read the Bible with greater satisfaction? Does not the truth fall upon your ear in the sanctuary with a different sound? Is not your love of the world checked? Are you not more disposed to seek the society of Christian people? Does not the subject of religion follow you to your place of business, and often come up unbidden to your mind? And yet you are "waiting for the Spirit!" What does all this mean, if it is not the Spirit moving upon your heart? While you are looking here and there for the Spirit, he is already within you. While, like Naaman and the prophet, you are expecting him to come and do some great thing for you, you hear not the still, small voice with which he is admonishing you to look to Christ and live. In occasional examples, he still approaches individuals, as he did Saul of Tarsus, and urges them into his kingdom with an impetuosity which leaves them no room to doubt, either as to the reality of the change in their condition, or the agency which has produced it. But these are exceptions to the established law of his administration. In ordinary cases, his first demonstration upon the heart is of a more tranquil character; and the entire process is apt to differ essentially from any thing which the individuals concerned may have anticipated. Enough to know that you are not to wait in passive idleness for the Spirit's aid. If you are willing to give up your sins, it is he who has made you willing. If you desire to come to Christ, that desire is from his silent influence upon your heart. Submit to his strivings; implore his further aid; and you will find the promise true, "To him that hath shall be given."

Here, in fact, is one of the great *encouragements* you have to enter at once upon a religious life. The seriousness of which you may even now be conscious, shows that God is mindful of you, and waits to bless you. For this state of feeling is not the fruit of chance. It is one of those good gifts which come down from above; a token of kindness; a harbinger of mercy. You may say of it, as Manoah's wife said to him, when he was expecting the Divine displeasure to break forth against them: "If the Lord were pleased to kill us, he would not have received a burnt-offering and a meat-offering at our hands, neither would he have showed us all these things, nor would, as at this time, have told us such things as these." If the Lord had not thoughts of peace toward you, would he have disturbed your spiritual slumber, and enkindled in your breast this solicitude about your soul? Or, if this language be too strong, would he have inclined you to reflect on your prospects for eternity, and to listen to the utterances of his word with an unwonted thoughtfulness? Here is the very Being knocking at your door, on whom your salvation depends. Can you need any further assurance of his readiness to save you?

Or, take a broader view of this question. You ask, What encouragement have I to seek an interest in Christ? The obvious and conclusive answer is to point you to the BIBLE. What is the Bible but a revelation of the Divine mercy to our world? "God so loved the world, that he gave his only-begotten Son, that whosoever believeth in him should not perish, but have everlasting life." "This is a faithful saying, and worthy of all acceptation, that Christ Jesus came into the world to save sinners." "Him that cometh unto me, I will in no wise cast out." What would you have more? What could you have? Here is a sacrifice of infinite cost, which God, of his own sovereign will, provided for the redemption of our race. Here is the distinct announcement that the grand object for which his beloved Son became incarnate, was to save sinners. And here is the gracious promise of the Saviour, that he will receive every sinner who comes to him. Are you prepared to say that God should have done more than this? It cannot be. The more you reflect upon it, the greater must be your astonishment that he should have done so much. Nor can you fail to see here the truth of the observation already made, that you have far more reason to hope for success in a diligent and prayerful search for salvation, than you have in prosecuting any mere secular plan whatever. But although you could not demand more at God's hand, he has actually given you more.

I refer now especially to the *character of the Saviour*. I mean by this, not his abstract ability to accomplish the work he has undertaken; that is implied in his being the co-equal of the Father, "God over all blessed forever." But I allude to his personal characteristics as exemplified in his teachings and actions. Take up the gospels, and study his life. Listen to his discourses. Place yourself by him while he performs his miracles. Go with him into the abodes of poverty and suffering. See with what compassion he deals with the sick and the sorrowful, the tempted and the erring. Behold what power a cry of distress has to arrest him on his journeys; how he accommodates himself to the weaknesses and the prejudices of different suppliants; how gently he reproves and instructs his ignorant and impetuous disciples; how tenderly he sympathizes with every stricken one who repairs to him for succour. All this is so much superadded to his boundless capacity to save sinners. It is omnipotence blended with meekness, and benevolence, and pity, and long-suffering, and tenderness beyond the yearnings of a mother's heart. It not only meets and countervails the sentiment of dread, which makes a sinful creature shrink from approaching the Creator, but it clothes the incarnate Deity with all those human attributes which usually win our affections and inspire our confidence. It diminishes unspeakably the difficulty of this work, that the Saviour is one who bears our nature, and has been tempted in all points as we are, and can, therefore, be touched with a feeling of our infirmities. You cannot but feel that there is every thing in his character to encourage your hopes; and the more so when you reflect, that during his earthly ministry, he never sent a sincere and humble suppliant away without a blessing.

But we may go a step further still in this direction. If the SAVIOUR'S character holds out encouragement to you, so also does the mission of the SPIRIT. We have just been speaking of his agency in another aspect. Consider it now as an incentive to resolute and persevering effort. So rigorous is the bondage sin has imposed upon us, that the crucifixion itself would have been ineffectual to our salvation, but for the ministration of the Spirit. His presence, however, obviates every difficulty. We are by nature blind to spiritual things, ignorant of ourselves, averse to holiness, inflated with ideas of our own goodness, devoted to the world, ashamed of Christ. If aroused to some degree of solicitude about our souls, we become painfully conscious of the strength of our depraved passions; the way of salvation appears obscure; we have no distinct apprehension of what we ought to do, and too often lack the moral courage to obey the dictates of our consciences. What with the turmoil of feeling within, and the subtle temptations which are sure to assail us from without, we are apt to conclude that the task to which we are summoned is too great for us, and must be given up or postponed to a more auspicious season. This insidious suggestion has its proper antidote in the doctrine of the Spirit's influence. The task laid upon you *is* beyond your strength. But what then? Does it exceed the resources of the omnipotent Spirit? Can not He who said, "Let there be light," dispel the darkness of your understanding? Can not He who reduced the primeval chaos to symmetry and beauty, restore harmony and peace to your agitated breast? This is his prerogative, and this his errand in our world. "When he, the Spirit of truth, is come, he shall guide you into all truth." It is his beneficent office to enlighten the mind; to banish its ignorance and prejudice; to show the sinner the worthlessness of his own righteousness as a foundation for his hopes; to make him sensible of his spiritual penury; to reveal to him the excellency and glory of the Redeemer, and to lead him a willing bondman to the Saviour's feet, with the feeling—

"Nothing in my hand I bring,
Simply to thy cross I cling;
Naked come to thee for dress,
Helpless look to thee for grace;

Vile, I to the fountain fly,
Wash me, Saviour, or I die."

This is what you need. It is all you need. And that Divine Spirit, who can accomplish this for you—who can teach you, strengthen you, renew you, guide you to Christ and fit you for heaven—is a God at hand, as well as a God afar off. His ministry is the great promise of the new dispensation. There is no blessing we have so much encouragement to pray for. We are even told that God is more willing to give the Spirit to those who ask him, than parents are to give good gifts to their children.

The whole ground of your hinderances and misgivings, therefore, is covered. Here is an almighty Spirit to conduct you, and an almighty Saviour to receive you. You have no difficulties from which they cannot extricate you;

no obstacles which they cannot enable you to surmount; no want which they cannot supply. If such proffers of aid were tendered you in any secular pursuit, how eagerly you would grasp at them! Are they of less value where your salvation is at stake?

But you may be unreasonable enough to hesitate still, because these are "abstract" promises; you would like to see them "tested," and then you could feel more confidence in venturing upon them. Well, *this* scruple is provided for. You have but to look around, and you can be gratified. There are witnesses on every side to testify, that they have proved these promises and found them true to the letter. They stood once where you stand, (for I am supposing that you have begun to "consider your ways.") They had the same doubts and fears, the same obscure views and fluctuating purposes. The world tempted them as it is tempting you. They formed resolutions and broke them. They were almost persuaded to be Christians, and then the shame of the cross overcame their fortitude. They determined to enter upon a new course of life, and the fear that they "might not persevere" made them draw back. But the Spirit continued to strive with them, until, at length, yielding to his benign solicitations, and relying upon his assistance, they gave themselves up to the Saviour with penitent and grateful hearts, and now they are "rejoicing in hope of the glory of God." Their faith rebukes your unbelief. The way of salvation is laid open to you as it was to them. You have the same warrant to accept of Christ's gracious invitation. You have the additional motives supplied by their experience. You have the sympathies and prayers of all Christian people. Your judgment is convinced. Your conscience is on the side of religion. The Spirit and the Bride bid you "Come." Why do you linger?

How extraordinary is it, that arguments and appeals like these should be necessary. Who is the party to be benefited? Whose salvation waits on these trembling balances? What measuring-line has sounded the depths of that abyss, what pen has depicted the glories of that paradise, between which your wavering spirit vibrates?

And yet you demand *encouragements* and *inducements* to begin a religious life, as though you were the party to confer the favour, and God to be the recipient of it! How amazing his forbearance, that even this ungrateful and (if the word must be used) arrogant state of mind, should not repel his clemency. He actually stoops to your caprices and gratifies your unreasonable exactions. He holds out "encouragements" to you far beyond any thing you could ask or expect. There is not an impediment in your way, not a difficulty you have to meet, for which he has not provided. And to crown the whole costly and elaborate system of relief which his munificence has prepared, his Spirit continues to strive with you. You may have tried to banish the subject of religion from your thoughts, and found yourself unequal to the task. Irksome as it may be, it cleaves to you with a tenacity you cannot overcome. Neither reading nor company, neither business nor pleasure, brings you relief. Thoughts of eternity rush upon you in the midst of your daily activities. They disturb you in the night-watches. The spiritual apathy of those around you cannot tranquillize your conscience. The sense of guilt haunts you, and the terrors of a coming judgment may oppress you, even while you are forcing yourself to appear cheerful. What is all this but the striving of the Spirit? the long-suffering of God, who is not willing you should perish, but rather that you should come to repentance?

Consider now what he has done for your salvation. Review the way in which he has led you. Ponder well the position you occupy. And see whether you can expect ever to be placed again in circumstances so favourable to your conversion. You cannot suppose either that God is indifferent to the manner in which you requite his gracious dispensations, or that his mercy is inexhaustible. While he offers us a free salvation, he cannot but view with abhorrence the deliberate and persevering rejection of his offer. The goodness displayed in redemption is infinite. And for such creatures as we are, to decline its benefits when he himself presses them upon our acceptance, betrays an ingratitude and a hardihood which cannot go unpunished. There is a limit, beyond which the Spirit will cease to strive. There is a point where mercy turns to vengeance. Your present thoughtfulness may warrant the hope, that you have not yet passed this fatal barrier. But you may be rapidly approaching it. Every thing may hang upon the issue of this conflict. While you are hesitating whether to cast yourself at the Saviour's feet, or to cleave a little longer to a world which is deceiving and ensnaring you, the hours may be hasting away, which are to fix your everlasting destiny. It should be enough to end this strife, that your salvation depends upon God, and that this appears to be *His* time. If Levi had not instantly left all when Christ called him, it is not probable he would ever have been made a disciple. If the three thousand on the day of Pentecost had not obeyed Peter's instructions, they might never have been converted. To trifle with serious impressions, is to insult God. To refuse to hear his voice when he is speaking directly to our heart, is to run the hazard of incurring that awful doom depicted in the book of Proverbs, (chapter 1st:) "Because I have called, and ye refused; I have stretched out my hand, and no man regarded; but ye have set at nought all my counsel, and would none of my reproof; I also will laugh at your calamity; I will mock when your fear cometh; when your fear cometh as desolation, and your destruction cometh as a whirlwind; when distress and anguish cometh upon you. Then shall they call upon me, but I will not answer; they shall seek me early, but they shall not find me; for that they hated knowledge, and did not choose the fear of the Lord; they would none of my counsel; they despised all my reproof. Therefore shall they eat of the fruit of their own way, and be filled with their own devices."

I have assumed, in the former part of this section, that the reader has been startled from his impenitency, and led to sober reflection. But, as has just been intimated, it would be too much to suppose, that this will be the case with all into whose hands this book may fall. Some among them will doubtless be as unwilling as ever, to take up the subject of religion, and consider it with the seriousness which it demands. To persons of this description, I feel at some loss what to say. Professing to know something of the ground you occupy, I have endeavoured with all the kindness which was compatible with fidelity to your souls, to exhibit the criminality of this inconsideration, to expose the sophistries by which it is usually palliated, to set forth your duty, and to show what ample encouragement God has given you to set about the performance of it. That we should have gone over all these topics without mitigating your aversion to the subject, is a fact of very painful significance. It is one of those facts which make men feel their impotence, in dealing with the depravity of the human heart. What a deep-seated enmity to God must possess the carnal mind, when it can stand out, not simply against the majesty and severity of the law, but against the boundless love and tenderness of the gospel! when it can even refuse to *consider* the claims of the Redeemer, to our confidence and veneration! And what must this import as to the moral condition of these persons? The apostle speaks of "tokens of perdition." It is a pregnant phrase. I will not say that it appertains to any reader of this volume. But you must judge for yourself, whether this confirmed inconsideration is not likely to prove, in your own case, a "token of perdition." Does it not look as though the spiritual insensibility, which has seized upon you, were to be invincible and permanent? Does it not seem like an omen of final and remediless ruin? I see not how any human agency is to prevent this result. Our only hope is in God. He can prevent it. But when the question is asked, Will he do this? every tongue must be mute. Secret things belong unto the Lord. We may not presume to pry into his counsels. One resource we have left—*prayer*. If your Christian friends have any proper love for your soul, they will be importunate in their intercessions for you. If you are not resolved upon self-destruction, I entreat you to pray for yourself. Peradventure, there may yet be mercy for you. The Father may even now wait to receive you. The Saviour may be stretching out his hand toward you, and crying, "Look unto me, and live."

The Holy Spirit may be secretly saying to you, "Awake, thou that sleepest, and arise from the dead, and Christ shall give thee light."

If you heed these gracious monitions, and, putting away all evasions and subterfuges, say with the prodigal, "I *will* arise and go to my Father," it will be well. Eternity will ratify the decision, and you will rejoice over it with a joy unspeakable and full of glory. But if you still refuse, and continue to reject the proffered mercy, I must again remind you that you tread on dangerous ground; for it is written, "My Spirit shall not always strive with man."

"There is a time, we know not when,
A point we know not where,
That marks the destiny of men
To glory or despair.

There is a line, by us unseen,
  That crosses every path;
The hidden boundary between
  God's patience and his wrath.

To pass that limit is to die,
  To die as if by stealth;
It does not quench the beaming eye,
  Or pale the glow of health.

The conscience may be still at ease,
  The spirits light and gay;
That which is pleasing still may please,
  And care be thrust away.

But on that forehead God has set
  Indelibly a mark,
Unseen by man, for man as yet
  Is blind and in the dark.

And yet the doomed man's path below
  May bloom as Eden bloomed:
He did not, does not, will not know,
  Or feel that he is doomed.

He knows, he feels that all is well,
  And every fear is calmed;
He lives, he dies, he wakes in hell,
  Not only doomed, but damned.

O where is this mysterious bourn
  By which our path is crossed;
Beyond which, God himself hath sworn,
  That he who goes is lost!

How far may we go on in sin?
  How long will God forbear?
Where does hope end, and where begin
  The confines of despair?

An answer from the skies is sent:
  "Ye that from God depart,
While it is called TO-DAY, repent,
  And harden not your heart."

SECTION V.

RELIGION MUST AND WILL BE CONSIDERED.

UP to this point, we have proceeded on the assumption, that it was *optional* with you, whether to consider the subject of personal religion or not. In this manner the Bible treats the question. It addresses us throughout as intelligent and responsible agents, and leaves us to decide on our own course after listening to its appeals and arguments. Your own conscience assures you that you can either choose or refuse to take up the plan of salvation, and examine it with a paramount reference to your own duty. God does not compel you to examine it. He commands, expostulates, invites, and points out the consequences involved in your disobedience. But he uses no coercion. You can still refuse. You often have refused. Instead of bringing your mind into contact with religion, when its claims were urged upon you, you have purposely directed it to something else. You have chosen rather to think of business or pleasure, or of any one of an endless variety of objects. It has not been at all to your taste to think about repentance and being born again, and renouncing the world and taking up the cross to follow Christ. And so you have shut these topics out of your breast and turned to more engaging themes. And thus far you have seen no very serious evil resulting from this habit;

for a habit it has become. Your inconsideration, you are apt to imagine, has not materially injured either your character or your prospects, and you are slow to believe there is so much danger attending it as has been represented. You are still disinclined, therefore, (for this is the case we are now to deal with,) to combat the repugnance you feel to spiritual religion, and to commence a new life.

Now, if this could last, there would be less room to remonstrate. You might be allowed to neglect religion just as long as your antipathy to it continued. I do not say that this would be wise, much less that it would involve no criminality. I speak only of safety. But it is of the highest moment for you to know that it cannot last. However your inconsideration may be a matter of option now, it will not be so always. There is a period coming, and it may be just at hand, when all discretionary control of this subject will be at an end, and you will be compelled to consider it. It belongs to the genius of the probationary dispensation under which we live, that no one should be *forced* into earnest and prolonged reflection upon the themes of the Bible. But "in the *latter days* ye shall consider it perfectly." On a death-bed it may be; certainly, after death, these august and solemn topics will engross your thoughts. They will gather around you then, not because they are more grateful than you find them now, nor because they are pressed upon you by more faithful and eloquent preachers. No preacher's voice will then be needed to awaken you to deep and anxious meditation. Nor will transitory impressions any more be obliterated, as so often happens with you here, by the returning waves of frivolity and worldliness. Alien as conviction of sin is from all your present tendencies and associations, it will then be your established condition. From never tolerating, much less fostering it, you will never be free from it. It will be your one dismal and terrible occupation, the very sum of your being, to dwell with sorrow and remorse upon those subjects which all the arguments of reason and Scripture, fortified by the warnings of Providence and the reproaches of conscience, cannot prevail upon you to admit into your bosom now.

It is due to you to place this fact distinctly before you. You should understand, that when the Scriptures exhort you to give attention to these subjects, and when the ministers of Christ enforce the exhortation with whatever skill or tenderness they can command, it is simply a question of time and place. It is as certain that you will be brought to consider them, as that you exist; and *that,* whatever your creed or character may be now. The whole solicitude of your Christian friends in urging the matter upon you is, that you may begin this work of consideration at once. They *know* you will do it sooner or later. And they know, with equal certainty, that every thing depends upon your doing it now.

If you ask what are the grounds of this representation, the answer is at hand. One of the chief reasons why you cannot be prevailed upon to apply your mind to the subject of religion is, that you are engrossed and captivated with worldly objects. At the period referred to, this temptation will be effectually removed. For "the heavens shall pass away with a great noise, and the elements shall melt with fervent heat, the earth also, and the works that are therein shall be burned up." This change virtually takes place with every individual at his death; for his relations with this world are then terminated, as really as though the globe should at that moment be destroyed. How fearful the transition must be to an unconverted sinner, no human pen may attempt to describe. But consider what is involved in being violently torn away from all the scenes and pursuits with which you are now occupied. When the claims of Christianity are pressed upon you, you turn to your business and your amusements, to your household cares, to your books, to your newspapers, to public events, to politics, and upon these interests you lavish the attention which is properly due to religion. Imagine yourself to be transported to some spot on the globe where none of these things would be within your reach—no business, no recreation, no reading, no cognizance of passing events, no opportunity for the exercise of ambition, of avarice, of enterprise, no means of personal culture, no congenial society; but, on the contrary, an unavoidable and intimate fellowship with companions scarcely removed from demons in character and behaviour. Can you picture to yourself any thing more horrible than this? And yet it would approximate only in the faintest degree to the actual condition upon which every unrenewed person enters at death. For the instant the soul quits the body, its severance from all things terrestrial is complete and final. There is not even left the spectacle of the earth itself to look upon; its sands and its seas, its herbage and its flowers, its forests and its mountains, all will have disappeared forever. How impossible will it be *then* for any man to drive away religion from his thoughts by inviting the world to come in and preoccupy them! The world, in so far as he is concerned, will have ceased to be. And, unless he has some other resource, for aught that the world can do for him, the unwelcome themes of religion will have undisputed possession of his breast.

This, however, is but a small part of the truth. Not only will he be cut off from all access to this world, but there will be every thing in his situation to force these repulsive topics upon his attention. Even here a rich man feels lost, if he is stripped of his wealth; and a scholar when deprived of his books; and a merchant when obliged to leave his business for a season; and a mother when separated from her children; and a child when removed from its parents, its school, or its play. But there, superadded to these privations, then become absolute and immitigable, there will be objects and associations too closely linked with eternal realities for the soul to elude or resist their influence. The rich man in the parable was taken up with his luxury, and feasting, and self-indulgence, until death snatched him away. Every one is ready to ask, what ensued after death. In this single instance, our Saviour has lifted the curtain and given us a glimpse of a lost soul after its discharge from the body. For although it is a parable, we cannot suppose that he would so construct it as to produce an impression upon our minds contrary to the truth. We follow this unconverted sinner, then, as the immortal spirit hastens away, and we find him presently "in hell, being in torments," and pleading with Abraham to send Lazarus, that he may dip the tip of his finger in water, and cool his tongue—for he was tormented in the flame. (Luke, chapter 16th.) We have no reason to doubt, that a similar doom, of which this may be but a faint and imperfect symbol, is experienced by every sinner dying in impenitency. And if this be so, you may judge whether it will be possible for one in these circumstances to avoid "considering" the serious topics which were so constantly repelled during this life. Will he be able to shut out the thought of eternity from his mind, now that he finds himself in eternity? Can he refuse to think of his soul, when his soul is disengaged from its clay tabernacle, and still preserves a conscious existence? Can he say in his heart "There is no God," when the vengeance of God is eating up his spirits? Can he treat hell as a chimera, when his ears have no respite from its weeping and wailing and gnashing of teeth? Can he flatter himself, that Christ is too compassionate to allow a sinner like him to perish, when the "*wrath of the Lamb*" is descending all around him, as "hailstones and coals of fire?" Oh, no, no! There will be no alternative left to you then. You will be compelled to think of religion. You will be no more able to thrust its solemn verities from you, than to compass your own annihilation.

So far from being allowed only an occasional and transient hearing, as they are here, they will cleave to you with an invincible tenacity, and fill up all your waking and your sleeping moments. Your sleeping moments, did I say? Alas, there will be no sleep for the lost soul. That is a night which brings no repose; a sorrow which knows no respite. Could the unhappy sinner cease from *thinking*, could he have even his intervals of mental torpor and forgetfulness, half the bitterness of his cup were gone. But this cannot be. He must think on, and think on, and think on; and *forever* think of the subjects which are most painful to him.

These subjects, I have said, are the great themes of religion, which are so often pressed upon your attention, and to so little purpose now. Of course you are not to infer from this that they will come up before the mind of a lost sinner in the same aspect as they do here. The invisible barrier which separates time from eternity, makes an infinite difference in the relations which we sustain to the Christian revelation and its Divine Author. So long as we are in this world, the Bible addresses us in accents of mercy. The very word gospel, like the Greek term of which it is the translation, means glad tidings. It is God's proclamation of pardon. It is a display of his benevolence and pity, which has filled all heaven with adoring wonder. It is a free tender of forgiveness and salvation to the very chief of sinners. And this proffer he continues to urge upon us, down to the very moment of death, by motives drawn from his own perfections, from the love of Christ, from the necessities of our own souls, from the ruined condition of the world, and from many other sources. But here he stops. The change which death produces in the outward condition of the impenitent sinner, is not greater than the revolution it effects in his relations to the system of redemption. To him, it ceases to be a system of redemption. There is no offer of pardon; no call to repentance; no striving of the Spirit. The Bible and the Sabbath, the ministry of reconciliation, and even the throne of grace, disappear. Instead of mercy there is judgment. For pity, there is vengeance. For "COME UNTO ME," there is "DEPART YE!" For the fountain opened for sin and uncleanness, there is the lake which burneth with fire and brimstone. All the objects which crowd upon the disembodied spirit breathe of retribution, and anguish, and despair. And every thing around and within conspires to fasten the thoughts, as by an inexorable necessity, upon that cross which has now ceased to be a symbol of mercy; and those abused privileges and warnings which come back with their scorpion stings to agonize the soul.

If it be disagreeable to you to think of religion here; if you have a conscious antipathy toward it when it is robed in light and loveliness, and seeks you out, only to extricate you from the toils of sin, and conduct you in triumph up to the realms of bliss, how will you bear the contemplation of it when it stands before you, arrayed in the terrors of vindicatory justice? If you cannot endure its offers of pardon and of heaven, how will you endure it when it forces itself upon you, as an ever-present, harrowing memorial, that those offers are withdrawn forever? If it is irksome to you to hear of Christ as a SAVIOUR, what would you not give to have the rocks and the mountains to fall on you and cover you, when the archangel's trump summons you to appear before him, as a JUDGE!

It would, perhaps, be some slight alleviation of the anguish of that day, were the whole race to encounter a common doom. So it will certainly aggravate the misery of the lost, to reflect, that to a portion of the race, this is a day of joy and triumph.

> "* * * * On the right hand of bliss,
> Sublime in glory, talking with their peers
> Of the incarnate Saviour's love,"

they will see a multitude which no man can number, who once dwelt with them in this vale of tears. Among them may be some whom they had known as neighbours, friends, fellow-worshippers, who sat side by side with them in the sanctuary, listened to the same sermons, sang the same hymns of praise, and united, outwardly at least, in the same prayers. Nay, there may be those who were bound to them by much more endearing ties,—a wife, a parent, a child, a sister, a household group, who used to sit around the same table, and with whose lives, theirs were interlaced like the reticulations of the vine, which spread its drapery over their family mansion. These are saved, and *they* are lost! They journeyed through life together, and at its close, they parted, never to meet, except as they meet now, one on the right hand of Christ, the other on his left; one never to weep, the other never to smile again. How inevitable and how poignant the conviction, that but for their own obduracy in refusing to come to Christ, they too might have been among that radiant company!

It will, indeed, be an overwhelming reflection, that they were fully instructed in their duty, and admonished of the consequences of neglecting it. Life and death were set before them. They knew, that unless they were born of the Spirit, they could not enter into the kingdom of God; that except they repented, they must perish; that if they refused to believe in Christ, they must be damned.* All this was distinctly presented to them. With many of them, it was instilled into their infant minds, and reiterated by pious parents, and

* John iii. 5. Luke xiii. 3. Mark xvi. 16.

proclaimed in their hearing by the ministers of the gospel, through the whole course of their lives. And if the consciousness that he once had "Moses and the prophets" augmented the suffering of the rich man in hell, what pangs of sorrow must they experience who had not only Moses and the prophets, but Christ and the apostles

> "*Ye knew your duty, but ye did it not!*
> These are the words to which the harps of grief
> Are strung; and to the chorus of the damned,
> The rocks of hell repeat them, evermore;
> Loud echoed through the caverns of despair,
> And poured in thunder on the ear of Wo."

There can be little hazard in saying to the reader of this treatise, that he knows his duty. It is not a thing of yesterday with you, that you have had access to the Bible, or that you have heard the preaching of the gospel. It has probably been your high privilege to grow up in the midst of religious influences, eminently adapted to direct your thoughts and efforts heavenward. So far from not being instructed in the essential doctrines and duties of Christianity, these may have been so vividly impressed upon your mind, that it has more than once cost you a struggle to stifle your convictions, and persist in your devotion to the world. Should you finally perish, (which may a merciful God prevent!) this fact cannot fail to impart new energy to every other element of your misery. It were in that case an unspeakable mitigation, could you be allowed to take your place at Christ's bar, with the people of Sodom and Gomorrah, with the besotted Hindoos, or with the ferocious cannibals of the South Seas. These must suffer; for they abused the light of nature. But nature is to the written revelation like a twinkling star to the sun; and all who pervert or neglect the Scriptures, must look for a corresponding retribution. There will be no wretchedness there, comparable to that of those who persevered through life, in counting the blood of the covenant an unholy thing, and doing despite to the Spirit of grace.

In the parable already mentioned, Abraham begins his reply to the lost sinner with a word of most pregnant signification. "Son, *remember!*" What unfathomable depths of sorrow are embosomed in this word! In this life you find it convenient, and therefore easy, to forget much that pertains to your spiritual well-being. You forget the pious lessons of the nursery. You forget the beneficent invitations of the Saviour. You forget the urgent expostulations of the sanctuary. You forget the serious meditations of the house of mourning. You forget the self-reproaches, and anxious prayers, and sacred promises of the bed of sickness. You forget the purposes of amendment so often formed, and the strivings of the Spirit so often resisted. But memory will be more faithful to its trust in that world. There are numerous facts which favour the belief, that nothing once confided to this mysterious faculty is ever lost. Instances have occurred of persons who have been able to recite long passages of the ancient classics, many years after they had lost all knowledge of the language, and of others who could commit to memory poems of great length in a language they never learned. There is a well-known case of a female servant, who, in a fit of delirium during sickness, was heard uttering Hebrew words and sentences: a marvel which was explained when an inquiry into her history brought out the fact, that she had once lived in the family of a learned German divine, whom she had heard reading and talking in Hebrew, as she was at work in his library. And several persons rescued from drowning have testified, that while struggling under the water, their past lives have come up before them with a vividness and minuteness of detail, which they could only describe by saying, "It seemed as though I thought of *every thing* I had ever said and done, or that had ever happened to me." These are fearful intimations as to the constitution of our being. They give plausibility to the conjecture, that the memory is like a book written over with sympathetic ink, which appears a blank until exposed to the fire, and then every page is seen covered with penmanship. Whatever vacuity may possess the mind of the unrenewed sinner when summoned before the bar of judgment, it is only necessary for the Judge to touch the secret spring of his memory, and his buried thoughts will start into being, "like the insects that come from an ant-hill when it is stirred." And can we doubt that God *will* do this? Is it not implied in the statement, that he "shall bring every work into judgment, with every secret thing, whether it be good or whether it be evil?" And are we not warranted in believing, that this transcript of the sinner's life, so comprehensive and so graphic as to reveal even his most secret thoughts, will not merely be spread before him at the last day, but *kept* before him by a too faithful memory throughout eternity? For myself, I cannot and do not doubt it.

And if it shall prove to be so, with how much reason may we contend, that those who refused to consider the subject of religion here, will be compelled to fasten their thoughts upon these unwelcome topics hereafter; and, most of all, upon the gracious dealings of God with them, and their base requital of his kindness. The life you have lived here, must be lived over and over again there. This religious education, these parental counsels and prayers, these providential warnings, these tranquil Sabbaths, these convictions of sin, these anxious forebodings about eternity, these resolutions of repentance, these secret cries for mercy, this shame of the cross, this fear of the world, these relapses into sin—all, all will recur hereafter, and continue to pass and repass before the mind, so long as the mind itself endures. You will think of God; but it will be as the Psalmist thought of him, "I remembered God, and was troubled." You will think of the Bible; but it will be as of a book which is now sealed against you. You will think of the Saviour; but it will be only to look on him whom you pierced, and whose blood now imprecates vengeance upon you. You will think of heaven; but it will be with the sad conviction that it was once within your reach, and is now separated from you by an impassable gulf. You will think of your Sabbaths; but it will be to reflect that they are gone forever. You will think of your seasons of religious anxiety; but it will be to remember, that when you were "almost persuaded to be a Christian," you dismissed the subject from your breast, and threw yourself again into the arms of an ungodly world.

"Wretch that I am!" you may well exclaim, "what shall I do, or whither shall I flee? I am weighed in the balance, and am found wanting. Oh, that I had never been instructed in the will of God at all, rather than that, being thus instructed, I should have disregarded and transgressed it. Would to God I had been allied to the meanest of the human race, to them that come nearest to the state of brutes, rather than that I should have had my lot in cultivated life, amid so many of the improvements of reason, and amid so many of the advantages of religion too! and thus to have perverted all to my destruction. Who can dwell in the devouring flames? Who can lie down in the everlasting burnings? But whom have I to blame in all this but myself? What have I to accuse but my own stupid and incorrigible folly? On what is all this terrible ruin to be charged, but on this one fatal cause, that, having broken God's law, I rejected his gospel too? And now my doom is sealed, and sealed forever."*

Would that I could spare you such a recital as this. It is not of choice, but of necessity that I present it. I shrink from this topic, the misery of a lost soul, with a repugnance which is wellnigh invincible. There is no theme so repulsive, so appalling to me; none that I so much dread to speak of. We are all liable to contract a subtle unbelief on this subject, which derives shelter and nourishment from our benevolent sympathies. There is something so horrible,

* Vide Doddridge's Rise and Progress.

so heart-rending in the thought, that one whom we have known and loved may pass out of this world into the abodes of the damned, and become the companion of the devil and his angels for all eternity, that we believe it as though we believed it not. We drive it away from us. We treat it as a phantom which must not be allowed to disturb our peace. But is this right? Is it wise? Is it becoming? Shall we aspire to be more merciful than the God of mercy? Are we to challenge to ourselves more tenderness than the Saviour? And did *he* avoid this subject? Did *he* refrain from speaking of "the worm that never dies and the fire that shall never be quenched?" It is the awful sanctity and the ineffable gentleness of his character which impart to his utterances on this topic so sublime a pathos, so unearthly a solemnity. No mistaken lenity kept him from proclaiming that there was a hell. Nor did he ever suppress the declaration, that it is the broad road, in which the mass of the race are walking, that leads to it. These truths concern us as deeply as they could the generation among whom he lived. And woe be to us if we deny or dissemble them. Yes, there *is* a hell. And every one who is neglecting the great salvation, is in imminent peril of it.

And now, the momentous alternative submitted to the reader is, Will you consider the subject of religion here, or will you consider it in eternity? One or the other you *must* do. You can no more elude it than you can cease to be. If you decline the examination of the subject here, "in the latter days you *shall* consider it perfectly." Judge for yourself, whether it will not be better, infinitely better, to give your attention to it now. In this world, religion contemplates you as a sinner ruined and condemned, but reprieved. It proposes itself to you as a system of mercy. It comes with the blood of atonement and the ministry of the Spirit, with pardon, and renewal, and holiness, and peace. It breathes of penitence and love, of hope and triumph, of a reconciled God and a glorious heaven. It finds you in circumstances in which you can comply with its demands, not only without compromising any of your interests, spiritual or secular, but with decided advantage to them all. It supplies you with every needful help—with a very profusion of the means of grace. It holds out to you encouragements and inducements to the performance of your duty, of the most engaging character. And it crowns all its appeals with a distinct and monitory exhibition of the fearful consequences which must attend your refusal.

Now, contrast with this, the situation in which you will be *compelled* to consider the subject, if it is neglected here. No longer in a world of probation, but in a world of retribution—the light of the Sun of righteousness, which is streaming down upon your pathway now, exchanged for the blackness of darkness—all your domestic ties and social affinities dissolved—all the plans and occupations which now engross you annihilated—religion presented to you only in its terrors—the Saviour known only in the dreadful *anathema* denounced against those who do not love him—the Spirit known only with the anguish of the sinner who has sinned away his day of grace—with no Bible to repair to for counsel—no friend to fly to for sympathy—no God to whom you can cry for mercy—no employments which can mitigate your desolation—no companions but such as will increase your wretchedness,—all possible forms and appliances of misery around you; and, *within*, the gnawings of the undying worm,—no respite, no peace, no hope—the remorse which knows no cessation—the despair which knows no ebb! And all this, forever—*forever*—FOREVER and EVER! Oh, my fellow-sinner, *can* you do this? Can you postpone all serious reflection to such a world? Can you pluck down upon yourself a ruin so awful, so irretrievable? Say not that this is an exaggerated picture, adapted only to harrow up the feelings. What pencil can depict the agonies of a lost soul? If you cannot bear to look upon the canvas, how could you *endure* the reality? And why will you run the hazard of it, by postponing your repentance? "He that being often reproved, hardeneth his neck, shall suddenly be destroyed, and that without remedy." Through the mercy of God, this doom, which so many others have encountered, has not yet overtaken *you*. You are still within sight of the cross. And the Saviour still bids you look to him and live.

> "Believe, and take the promised rest;
> Obey,—and be forever blest!"

SECTION VI.

WHAT CAN I DO?

I AM willing to believe, that among the readers of this book, there may be, here and there, one upon whom the arguments and appeals presented in the preceding pages will not have been thrown away. You are at length satisfied, that it is your duty to attend to the claims of personal religion. But the subject is so new and strange to you that you know not how to go about it. "I would like to become a Christian. But what can I do? *Tell me just what to do,* and I am ready to follow your directions." This is your language. If it is uttered in good faith, (as I, of course, presume it to be,) it is cause for thankfulness. It is a great point gained, when an individual has been brought by the Spirit of God to that state of mind, that he is disposed to ask, "What must I do to be saved?"

The answer to this momentous question has been interwoven with the whole texture of this volume, and, in several places, stated in a formal way. But your desire for a more particular explanation of the subject is reasonable, and shall be complied with, so far as God may enable me to meet your wishes.

Let us first review the plan of salvation. This very phrase, as you will perceive, directs the mind to our *lost* condition; for he only who is lost, requires to be saved. The ruin in which we were overwhelmed by the apostacy of our first parents, comprises two distinct but inseparable parts or elements: depravity of heart, and subjection to the penalty of the Divine law. The former is set forth in such passages as these: "That which is born of the flesh is flesh." "By nature, the children of wrath." "Every imagination of the thought of man's heart is only evil continually." "All have sinned and come short of the glory of God." "The carnal mind is enmity against God." "The heart is deceitful above all things, and desperately wicked."* The other characteristic of our ruined state is affirmed with equal explicitness. "The wages of sin is death." "The wrath of God is

*John iii. 6. Eph. ii. 3. Gen. vi. 5. Rom. iii. 23; viii. 7. Jer. xvii. 9.

revealed from heaven against all ungodliness and unrighteousness of men." "Cursed is every one that continueth not in all things which are written in the book of the law to do them." "The soul that sinneth, it shall die."* A reference Bible will direct you to numerous other passages, bearing on each of these points. The doctrine they teach is, that man is by nature and by practice a guilty and helpless sinner. His depravity extends to all his powers; his understanding is darkened; his affections are earthly and grovelling; his will is rebellious; his conscience is enfeebled or perverted, and the whole current of his being, instead of tending toward his Creator, is alien from God, and hostile to his character and government.

* Rom. vi. 23; i. 18. Gal. iii. 10. Ezek. xviii. 4

Of course, he is under condemnation. The sentence of the law has gone out against him, and retributive justice waits to visit him with its penal curse.

It is evident, (as formerly intimated,) that the only salvation which can meet the exigencies of a race in this condition, must be of the twofold character of the misery from which they are to be extricated. To employ a familiar illustration, the sinner is in the condition of a criminal, who, while under sentence of death, is attacked with a mortal disease. There are two things which a man in these circumstances needs, neither of which will avail him any thing without the other. He may receive a pardon, but he will still die of his malady. He may be healed of his malady, but he will have to suffer for his crime. He must be both healed and pardoned, or his life is gone. So with the sinner. He requires to be forgiven, and to be cured of the fatal leprosy of sin. Forgiveness alone would not fit him for heaven. Neither would spiritual healing. The two must be combined. And in the economy of redemption they are combined. One of them is secured in the renewing of the heart by the Holy Spirit; the other, by the soul's casting itself upon the Lord Jesus Christ, to be pardoned and accepted, solely through the merit of his atoning blood and perfect righteousness.

These themes are the burden of the New Testament. "Except a man be born again, he cannot see the kingdom of God." "Of his own will begat he us with the word of truth." "If any man be in Christ, he is a new creature; old things are passed away; behold, all things are become new." "Except ye repent, ye shall all likewise perish." "God so loved the world, that he gave his only-begotten Son, that whosoever believeth in him should not perish, but have everlasting life." "Christ is the end of the law for righteousness, to every one than believeth." "Him that cometh unto me, I will in no wise cast out." "For he hath made him to be sin for us who knew no sin, that we might be made the righteousness of God in him." "Even the righteousness of God, which is by faith of Jesus Christ unto all, and upon all them that believe, for there is no difference." "He that believeth on him is not condemned; but he that believeth not is condemned already, because he hath not believed in the name of the only-begotten Son of

God." "Holiness, without which no man shall see the Lord."*

In these and other passages, it is sometimes regeneration, sometimes justification, and again, faith, or repentance, or holiness, which is declared to be indispensable to salvation. All are alike necessary; and are equally included or implied in the work of the Spirit within us, and the work of the Saviour *without* us. In the statement just made, I have substituted the word "justification" for "pardon" or "forgiveness," previously used. The reason is, that man needs more than pardon; he must be "justified." When a convict is pardoned, he is simply set free from the penalty of

* John iii. 3. James i. 18. 2 Cor. v. 17. Luke xiii. 3. John iii. 16. Rom. x. 4. John vi. 37. 2 Cor. v. 21. Rom. iii. 22. John iii. 18. Heb. xii. 14.

the law. If his sovereign should also invite him to his palace, adopt him as a son, exalt him to the highest honours of the realm, and make over to him a title in perpetuity to his kingdom, it would supply an illustration of what God is pleased in his infinite mercy to do for every penitent and believing sinner; and of what, it may be added, *must* be done in order to his salvation.

But you will ask, with anxiety, How is this effected? I answer, Through the mediation of our Lord Jesus Christ. As is clearly set forth in the Scripture testimonies that have been quoted, our condition by nature was quite hopeless. In so far as any resources of our own, or of other races of creatures, were concerned, we must have remained forever under the power of that penal death which is the righteous penalty of the

Divine law. But "where sin abounded, grace hath much more abounded." God was pleased, of his mere good pleasure, to send his only-begotten Son into the world, that we might live through him. Uniting our nature with his own, Jesus stooped to become our SUBSTITUTE, and to expiate our sins with his blood. Assuming our law-place, he rendered to the law that obedience which we had failed to render, and bore that penalty which we had incurred. It was a fundamental principle of the Divine administration, that "without shedding of blood, there could be no remission." The shedding of CHRIST'S blood not only sustained, but "magnified" the law; while it illustrated, beyond any other measure of which it is possible for the human mind to conceive, the dreadful evil of sin, and the boundless love, the inflexible justice, and the immaculate holiness of the Deity. It was as our SURETY he suffered and died. "He bore our sins in his own body on the tree." "While we were yet sinners, Christ died for us." "Ye are redeemed with the precious blood of Christ." "Christ hath redeemed us from the curse of the law, being made a curse for us."

On the *efficacy* of this sacrifice there can be no question. It was appointed and accepted by the Father; and the least consideration of the subject must suffice to show, that the blood of such a victim has a value sufficient to atone for the sins of unnumbered worlds, if it were the purpose of God so to apply it.

Here, then, is what every sinner needs, — what *you* need, — a sacrifice which takes away sin, and a righteousness which fulfils all the requirements of the Divine jurisprudence. How can they so become *your's* as to avail to your justification? The answer which the Scriptures give to this important question, is—by FAITH. "He that *believeth* on the Son hath everlasting life; he that believeth not the Son shall not see life, but the wrath of God abideth on him." "God is just, and the justifier of him that *believeth* in Jesus." "This is his commandment, that we should *believe* on his Son Jesus Christ." This act is in other places styled, a looking to Christ, receiving Christ, building on Christ, and, more commonly, coming to Christ. For all practical purposes, these expressions may be regarded as equivalent and interchangeable. The sinner, enlightened by the Spirit and word of God, is made sensible of his depraved and miserable condition, of his exposure to the Divine displeasure, and of the worthlessness of his former hopes; and, discovering at the same time the excellency and sufficiency of CHRIST, he receives and rests upon him alone for salvation. In other words, he *believes* the testimony of God concerning his own sin and ruin. He *believes* His testimony concerning Jesus Christ, as the propitiation for our sins, our Ransom, and our suffering and atoning High Priest. He *believes* the gracious assurance, that God will save to the uttermost all who come unto him by Jesus Christ; that none who come shall in any wise be cast out; that "every one who thirsteth," yea, that "whosoever will," even though he be the chief of sinners, may come to Christ, and shall be made welcome. This he believes;—not, indeed, without much distrust and many a conflict; and not, ordinarily, without having tried various fruitless expedients for obtaining peace of mind. But, in the end, he *believes* it; and thereupon, with contrition for his sins, and gratitude for the boundless mercy of God, he accepts the revealed method of salvation, and *trusts* in the merits of Christ as the foundation of his hope. Relying upon the righteousness of Christ for acceptance, that righteousness is made over to him or set down to his account—precisely as our sins were laid upon the Saviour. As our Substitute, he consented to be "made sin for us," that is, to have our sins visited upon him, and to be regarded and treated as a sinner in our stead. And his compassionate design in this was, that "we might be made the righteousness of God in him;" to wit: that his righteousness (his "obedience unto death," whereby he fully satisfied the claims of the law) might be so reckoned to our account, that we should be regarded and treated as righteous; or, in other words, be "justified." It is this closing in with the gospel method of salvation, this cordial assent of the soul to Christ's invitations, this entire surrender of the heart to him, not only as a SAVIOUR to be trusted in, but as a KING and SOVEREIGN, to be obeyed and honoured, which constitutes true faith. And if *you* thus believe in Christ, you will be saved.

"But what," you may be ready to ask, "becomes of *regeneration* and *repentance*. Are not these also essential to salvation?" They are. But will you recur to the views presented in a former part of this Treatise, on the nature of the Spirit's work upon the heart? This

Divine agent, we have reason to believe, not only presents the truth to the mind, but, in some mysterious manner, operates directly upon the mind, so as to enable it to *apprehend* the truth in its just import. He imparts, with the light, the capacity of spiritual vision. (See 1 Cor. ii. 14.) But all this is done without trenching upon our free agency. The sinner acts with as perfect *freedom* in every stage of his conversion—and in the entire development and growth of the spiritual man—as he ever did in rejecting the Saviour, or in prosecuting a secular project. But the Almighty Spirit is there, gently withdrawing the scales from his eyes, unveiling to him his real condition, disclosing the majesty of the violated law, the awful holiness of the Godhead, and the efficacy of the great sacrifice, swaying his reluctant will, loosening his hold upon the world, and, by degrees, leading him on, in penitence, and doubt, and anxiety, toward the cross—and, at length, to the Saviour himself. It is *while* you are "striving to enter in at the strait gate," and occupied with looking to Christ, and as the *cause* of your doing this, that the Spirit is "working in you to *will* and to do of his good pleasure." And it is through the efficacy of his renewing grace that you do, as the first act of the new life he has imparted to you, open your heart to Jesus of Nazareth, and cry, "My Lord and my God!"

The exercises which *precede* this receiving of Christ are endlessly diversified. "By the law is the knowledge of sin." "The law is our school-master to bring us to Christ." And the "law-work" (as the old divines expressed it) is longer or shorter, milder or more pungent, in different cases. In most of the examples of conversion recorded in the New Testament, it was of brief duration. Witness the dying thief; the three thousand; the jailer of Philippi; the Roman converts. (Acts xxviii.) In some cases, there was intense anxiety and terror, as with the jailer and the publican. While in others, there seems to have been no convulsion of feeling whatever, but an humble and grateful reception of a crucified Saviour as soon as he was made known: to this class may be referred the instances of the centurion, (Luke vii.,) the Ethiopian eunuch, (Acts viii.,) and Lydia, (Acts xvi.) The same diversity has obtained in later times. Luther was a long while groping his way to the cross—no strange thing certainly, when we consider the circumstances in which he was placed. This also was the experience of Bunyan, and of that great man, Dr. Owen; both of whom passed through protracted and painful conflicts. But in numerous other cases of undoubted conversion, there has been a close resemblance to those Scriptural examples, in which the soul was drawn to the Saviour with cords of love.

Nothing is more common than for individuals newly aroused to serious reflection, to insist upon a specific measure of "conviction," as an essential prerequisite to their coming to Christ. That some degree of conviction is demanded, appears from the fact, that no one will seek a Saviour until he feels himself to be lost. "They that are whole need not a physician, but they that are sick." But the precise extent to which this law-work shall be carried in any given case depends on the sovereignty of God. If Jesus sees fit to send a word, in passing, to the heart of Matthew, sitting at the receipt of custom, which shall *instantaneously* transmute him into a disciple; and to consign Saul of Tarsus to three days and nights of blindness and contrition and remorse; neither may complain—Saul, that he experienced too much distress, nor Matthew that he experienced too little. The most intense mental anguish has no *merit* in it. And the ardent desire for it, on the part of awakened sinners, frequently springs from a subtle spirit of self-righteousness—from a feeling that it would in some way *recommend* them to the Saviour, or move his pity toward them. How fallacious this idea is, might be seen from the fact that individuals sometimes experience the most torturing convictions, without being converted. Of what avail were the convictions of Cain—of Judas—of Felix? Nor is it less important to observe, that the feeling of which I am now speaking, is derogatory to the Saviour. It aims at the securing to the sinner himself a share in the glory of his salvation. He would come to Christ with a price in his hand—deeming himself not altogether unworthy of his clemency, *because* of his tears and his self-reproaches and his mental anguish. Distressed and humbled he may well be: if he could see his sins in all their enormity, his remorse and terror would far exceed any thing he has yet experienced. But there is no merit in this. It has no efficacy to expiate the least of his transgressions. It cannot, in the slightest degree, mitigate his ill-desert. And so long as he trusts in it to make himself *less unworthy* to be accepted and saved, it will prove an invincible barrier to his coming to Christ at all. If we are ever saved, it must be by coming to Christ as miserable, depraved, ruined, and helpless sinners, without righteousness and without strength, feeling that *all* the merit must be his, that his blood alone can cleanse us, and that it is for God, in his wise and holy sovereignty, to decide, whether we shall be sprinkled with that precious blood, or left to perish. It is to those who are soothing themselves with a complacent self-righteousness, which as often assumes the type just indicated, as any other, he says, "Because thou knowest not that thou art wretched, and miserable, and poor, and blind, and naked, I counsel thee to buy of me gold tried in the fire, that thou mayest be rich; and white raiment, that thou mayest be clothed, and that the shame of thy nakedness do not appear; and anoint thine eyes with eye-salve, that thou mayest see."

It may be, that amid the variety of topics which offer themselves for consideration in examining this vital question, you find your mind confused. Let me say then, that the duty of one who desires, without longer delay, to make his peace with God, is perfectly simple and plain. It is defined in that expression so often cited, "COME UNTO ME, and I will give you rest." You have but this *one thing* to do. You need not (now) perplex yourself with inquiring, whether the Spirit has changed your heart; nor whether your repentance is yet deep enough to "authorize" you to believe in Christ; nor whether your motives in desiring to be saved are altogether pure; nor with any thing else pertaining to your own exercises. Your warrant, your sole warrant, for coming to Christ, is contained in his word, not in your feelings. It is as much addressed to you as to any other human being; as much as it was to any one among the myriads who have appropriated it and found mercy. It is well to examine your heart by the light of Scripture, to review your life, and to lay to heart the years that have been spent in impenitence, and the mercies that have been abused; but the *exclusive* contemplation of these things will divert your thoughts from the Saviour. And it is in *looking to Christ* that the sinner soonest learns to appreciate the evil of sin, the baseness of his ingratitude, and his infinite obligations to redeeming mercy. This, in fact, is genuine repentance; the repentance which flows from a discovery of the divine *mercy,* in connection with the purity and spirituality of the moral law. "They shall look upon ME whom they have pierced, and they shall mourn." It is when the sinner has been led by the Holy Spirit to the Saviour; when he looks upon him he has pierced, and beholds the Lamb of God which taketh away the sin of the world, that he abhors himself, and repents in dust and ashes. Then it is he sorrows after a godly sort; sorrows, not because he dreads the punishment of sin, but because he feels the intrinsic evil of sin, and sees that it has been committed against a God of infinite goodness, who has been all his life loading him with blessings. Here is the repentance which is unto life; and it is so far from being restricted, as "inquirers" are apt to suppose, to the dawn of religion in the soul, that it forms an essential part of the daily experience of the Christian, until he exchanges his body of sin and death, for the beatific life of heaven. It should be added, too, that in many cases, as with President Edwards, Christians experience far more humbling and affecting discoveries of their deep depravity in after years, than they did at their conversion.

If these views are correct, the question which now concerns the reader, is, ARE YOU WILLING TO COME TO CHRIST? Do you see and feel yourself to be, by nature and by practice, a lost and helpless sinner? Is it your earnest desire and purpose, God helping you, henceforth to hate and forsake all sin? Are you ready to give up the world, that is, the supreme love of the world, and devotion to its interests, for the love and service of God? Have you seen the insufficiency of your own morality, of your orthodox creed, your hereditary faith, your reformation, your contrition, your prayers, your religious observances, to entitle you to forgiveness, or recommend you to the divine compassion? Are you prepared to renounce all dependence upon these things, and to cast yourself upon the mercy of God in Jesus Christ, to be washed from your sins in his blood, to be justified only through his righteousness, and henceforth to wear his yoke, to own him as your Lord, and to spend the remainder of your life in his service? If you can answer these questions in the affirmative, what hinders that you should *now* come to Christ, and receive him as your all in all? "Unworthy," you doubtless are; but who ever came to Christ, being *worthy?* The feeling of "worthiness" would actually exclude you from his offer: for he "came not to call the righteous, but sinners to repentance." If you come to him at all, it must be *just as you are.* Here is the way in which you must come; described so well, that I see not how any uninspired pen, could describe it better:—

"Just as I am—without one plea,
But that thy blood was shed for me,
And that thou bidd'st me come to thee—
O Lamb of God, I come!

"Just as I am, and waiting not
To rid my soul of one dark blot—
To thee, whose blood can cleanse each spot,—
O Lamb of God, I come!

"Just as I am, though tossed about
With many a conflict, many a doubt,
Fightings within, and foes without—
O Lamb of God, I come!

"Just as I am—poor, wretched, blind:
Sight, riches, healing of the mind,
Yea, all I need in *Thee* to find,—
O Lamb of God, I come!

"Just as I am, thou wilt receive,
Wilt welcome, pardon, cleanse, relieve,
Because thy promise I believe—
O Lamb of God, I come!

"Just as I am—thy love unknown
Has broken every barrier down;
Now to be thine, yea, *thine alone*—
O Lamb of God, I come!"*

I anticipate the feeling with which some of my readers may listen to this representation. "I would *like* to feel thus, but I do not. I am willing to do any thing which may inspire me with these feelings, and aid me in coming to Christ. What am I to do?" I reply,

*I learn through a private channel, that this beautiful Hymn was written by Miss ELLIOT, of Torquay, England.

that the commands of God and his gracious invitations, call for an *immediate* compliance. All things are ready. The Saviour bids you look to him, and live. The present is his time: it should be yours. Such are the uncertainties and perils of life, that a single day's delay may transfer this question from a world of hope to a region of despair. I urge you then to go to Christ "just as you are," without an hour's procrastination. But if you still ask, "What can I do to increase the interest I begin to feel in this momentous subject, and to assist me in entering upon a Christian life?" I answer, by suggesting *again* the following things, which you *can* and *should* do.

1. *You can deliberately make up your mind as to the duty* of attending to the subject of religion at this time. Count the cost of doing it. (Luke xiv. 25–33.)

And determine, as the grace of God may enable you, whether you will from this time make it your paramount concern, to seek an interest in the blood of Christ, and to serve him.

2. *You can faithfully exert yourself to put away all known sin.* You may be free from gross vices, but you can not be free from sin. You may be proud, or vain — ambitious— passionate—petulant —resentful—avaricious—deceitful—censorious—or addicted to levity and foolish jesting.* You may have slidden into

* "Foolish jesting." It is not sufficiently considered, how hostile this habit is to serious reflection. There are persons who make it their vocation to say witty things. They are looked to in all companies to make the fun. Like the king's fool at the ancient courts, they are expected to turn every thing into ridicule; and, conscious of their calling, they are perpetually essaying puns and pleasantries.

unworthy practices in your business. You may be excessively fond of gay amusements, and the frivolities of fashionable life. You may be chargeable with the habitual desecration of the Sabbath; at least, in the way of neglecting its ordinances. It is impossible to cover this ground by an enumeration of specific sins. But take the decalogue, and, with the assistance of any good exposition, (such as the commentaries and catechisms supply,) endeavour to

---

Not to comment on this practice as a matter of *taste*, about which opinions might differ, there can be no question that it is most unfriendly to religious thoughtfulness. The individual who is so unfortunate as to be addicted to it, will find it a great impediment to his salvation. His good purposes will speedily succumb to his levity; and he may barter his soul for the paltry reputation of a humorist.

discover to what sins you are prone. And, looking upward for help, begin at once to forsake and watch against them. Many persons appear to suppose that it will be time enough to put away their sins, and discharge every known duty, after they shall have become Christians. This is not the way to be saved. "Turn yourselves, and live ye." (Ezek. xviii. 32.) "Let the wicked forsake his way, and the unrighteous man his thoughts, and let him return unto the Lord, and he will have mercy upon him; and to our God, for he will abundantly pardon." (Isaiah lv. 7.) The first thing to be done, is to forsake your evil way, and even your evil "thoughts." Any unwillingness to do this may well lead you to distrust your own sincerity in professing a desire to enter upon a religious life. There is no more decisive characteristic of one who is really "striving to enter in at the strait gate," than a careful and humble watching against all sin, whether in thought, word, or deed.

3. As closely allied to the counsel just given, *you can,* to a considerable extent at least, *avoid scenes and associations which are hostile to serious reflection.* Religious thoughtfulness is too much an exotic in your breast to thrive without being sheltered and nurtured. It may be impaired, and possibly extinguished, by frivolous talking, by gay amusements, by light reading. Nay, the very shame of the cross, and the stifling of convictions, (Mark viii. 38, John xii. 42, 43,) may efface your impressions.

4. While shunning these adverse influences, *you can court those of an opposite character,* which will fortify you in your good purposes, and aid you in your ef-

forts. Pre-eminent among these are the services of the sanctuary, both on the Sabbath and during the week. I mention the last because of the repugnance you may have felt to going to a weekly lecture or prayer-meeting. There is a feeling on this point among many persons, as irrational as it is pernicious. *You* certainly, if you are in earnest in seeking your salvation, will not disparage these social religious meetings. You will gladly avail yourself of the valuable assistance you can derive from them in the way of subduing the worldliness of your spirit, emancipating you from the bondage of things visible and transitory, and bringing you into a closer fellowship with Christian ordinances and Christian people. It is well to breathe the atmosphere of a house of prayer. It is in the sanctuary, too, that God's truth is published and explained; and there the omnipotent Spirit most frequently works his miracles of mercy in the conversion and salvation of sinners.

5. *You can devote a portion of every day to the devout reading of the Scriptures, and other religious books.* Of such vital importance is this, that it would be impossible to insist upon it too strongly. It was by the study of the Bible he found in the convent of Erfurt, that Luther was gradually led into the truth, and so, in the end, equipped for the Reformation. The Rev. Thomas Scott, the Commentator, whose praise is in all the churches, commenced his ministry in the established Church of England, as a decided Socinian. And it was through the blessing of God on his private study of the Scriptures, that he became, some

years after, an able expounder and defender of the faith he had once destroyed. The "FORCE OF TRUTH," the narrative in which he has portrayed the struggles of his powerful intellect in escaping from the bondage of error, is one of the most interesting and instructive books of our Christian literature; and you would do well to read it. The radiant career of Mr. Wilberforce as a Christian statesman, is to be traced, under God, (remotely at least,) to his perusal of the Greek Testament with his friend, the Rev. Isaac Milner, as they travelled together from England to Nice.

These cases, which might easily be multiplied, illustrate the importance of a diligent study of the Scriptures. The entrance of God's word giveth light. The Holy Scriptures "are able to make thee wise unto salvation." You will not study them in vain. Let your reading, for the present, be *chiefly* in the New Testament, with the book of Psalms. You will probably find it profitable to take up one of the Gospels, say the Gospel of John, and read it continuously. In connection with it, read some of the Epistles, say Philippians, Hebrews, 1 Peter and 1 John; and then other portions, both of the New Testament and the Old. A judicious Commentary, like Scott or Henry, may be of essential service to you. And whether you use a commentary or not, the examination of parallel passages, as indicated in the reference Bibles, will throw a great deal of light on the sacred text, and present familiar truth to your mind in new and engaging aspects.

With the reading of the Scriptures, you should have in hand some other suitable books. I know of none more appropriate than those mentioned in a former section.* To these may be added, the Pilgrim's Progress, Newton's Letters, Jay's Morning and Evening Exercises, Baxter's Call, and his Saints' Rest, Dr. J. W. Alexander's Thoughts on Family Worship, James's Anxious Inquirer, Henry's Anxious Inquirer, Memoir of Dr. Gordon, (or the "Christian Philosopher triumphing over death,") and the lives of Luther, Bunyan, Henry Martyn, Wilberforce, Hannah More, Alexander, Payson, Neff, McCheyne, and others of kindred character. Books of this sort will be almost certain to fix your attention: your mind will be kept *in contact* with religion; and the more you read, the more will your *feelings* become enlisted in the subject.

* Vide pp. 108, 109.

6. *You can confide your views to some kind and judicious Christian friend*—and with great advantage. This is a point where many stumble. A sinful pride puts them upon concealing their thoughtfulness *until* they shall have become established in the hope of the gospel: *then* they mean to lay aside all disguise. The too common effect of this is, to smother and destroy their seriousness altogether. You surely have some friend in whom you can trust,—your pastor, if no one else; and you could not gratify him more than by going to him on such an errand. Give him the opportunity, and he will explain many things which may perplex you. He will point out your mistakes and dangers. He will sympathize with you in your trials and temptations. And although he can do nothing effectual for you, but simply

say, with John the Baptist, "BEHOLD THE LAMB OF GOD, WHO TAKETH AWAY THE SIN OF THE WORLD!" yet he may do *this* in such a way as shall, by the divine blessing, greatly help you in finding the road to the cross.

7. I waive various other points, to say, in conclusion, *you can pray*. And pray you must, if you would be saved. Pray you will, if you are not practising self-deception. I mention this last, because it must be *combined* with all the other duties which have been specified, or they will be nugatory. Without prayer you can neither put away your sins, nor shun evil associations. Without prayer, the services of the sanctuary may but harden you; the private study of the Bible will be dry and repulsive; and the counsels of Christian friendship will fall upon reluctant ears. We have not the

slightest reason to expect that we shall ever understand the gospel, or ever be renewed, or pardoned, or *saved*, without prayer. There is nothing more indispensable; nothing which promises more affluent returns. It is one of the endearing titles of the Deity, the Hearer of Prayer. (Ps. lxv. 2.) We are everywhere exhorted to pray. "Seek ye the Lord while he may be found; call ye upon him while he is near;"—a command addressed to those who are immediately told, "Let the *wicked* forsake his way," etc. (Isa. lv. 6, 7.) "Then shall ye call upon me, and ye shall go and pray unto me, and I will hearken unto you. And ye shall seek me, and find me, when ye shall search for me with all your heart." (Jer. xxix. 12, 13.) "Men ought *always* to pray, and not to faint." "Ask, and it shall be given you." (See the whole passage, Matt. vii. 7–11. See also Phil. iv. 6. 1 Thess. v. 17. Heb. iv. 16. James i. 5. 1 John v. 14, 15.)

Among the promises connected with prayer, that of the *Spirit's influence* is pre-eminent. (See Luke xi. 13.) As there is no blessing we so much need, so there is none which is so freely promised. Let this be your encouragement. The Holy Spirit can do for you *all* that you require. He can remove all your difficulties on points of doctrine. He can guide you into the truth. He can resolve all your questions of duty. He can preserve you from self-deception. He can awaken in your breast an ingenuous sorrow for sin. He can take away your heart of stone, and give you a heart of flesh. He can unveil to you the glorious character of the Redeemer, and lead you, a willing and joyful captive, to his feet. He can transform you into a new creature in Christ Jesus, make you as holy as you have been corrupt, prepare you for heaven, and bring you there. Are not these blessings worth praying for?

It is of no avail to say, that you are not yet "good enough" to pray; that your heart is too callous; that you could not pray with "pure motives;" and that God would not hear your prayers. All these are the suggestions of pride and unbelief. It is setting up your own caprices, or, at least, your own misconceptions, against the clear authority of God. It is impossible for you to examine the Scripture testimonies on this subject, with any degree of candour, without perceiving that he has made it the imperative duty of *every one* to pray; and that you have no reason to look for his blessing, except in answer to prayer. Besides, if the corrupt state of your heart, the selfishness of your motives, and the ascendency of the world over you, disqualify you for praying, when are these obstacles to be removed? and *how?* It is just the case of a sick man waiting to cure himself, before he sends for a physician. Undoubtedly, it is that "evil heart of unbelief" which constitutes the grand hinderance to your salvation, and which makes it impossible for you, not only to pray aright, but to read the Scriptures aright, to hear the preaching of the gospel aright, or to do any thing else in such a manner as to receive the approval of a holy God. But what are you to do? Will you shut up your Bible, will you absent yourself from the sanctuary, will you cease from all further efforts to secure your salvation, because you are too sinful to do these things as they ought to be done? You cannot but see the sophistry of this pretext. It is *because* you are full of sin, you ought to *pray*. Pray as the publican did. Pray as the dying thief did. Pray as the father of the demoniac child did: "Lord, I believe: help thou mine unbelief." Pray thus, and continue praying, and you will not pray in vain.

To imagine that you have no right to pray in your present condition, is a sheer illusion. You have no right to abstain from praying. To suppose that it could do you no good, is a kindred mistake. Try the experiment. Unfit as you feel yourself to be for it; conscious that your heart is still selfish and worldly; ashamed, it may be, to look up to God, and take his name upon your lips; make the effort. These very impediments only show how much you *need* to pray. And it will surprise and encourage you to find how certainly they will yield to earnest and habitual prayer.

Such, then, is the answer to your inquiry, "*What can I do to become more deeply interested in religion?*"

YOU CAN DELIBERATELY MAKE UP YOUR MIND, AS TO THE DUTY OF ATTENDING TO THE CLAIMS OF RELIGION. YOU CAN FAITHFULLY EXERT YOURSELF TO PUT AWAY ALL KNOWN SIN. YOU CAN, TO A CERTAIN EXTENT, AVOID SCENES AND ASSOCIATIONS WHICH ARE HOSTILE TO SERIOUS REFLECTION. YOU CAN COURT SUCH INFLUENCES AS ARE OF AN OPPOSITE CHARACTER. YOU CAN DEVOTE A PORTION OF EVERY DAY TO THE DEVOUT READING OF THE SCRIPTURES AND OTHER RELIGIOUS BOOKS. YOU CAN CONFIDE YOUR VIEWS TO SOME KIND AND

JUDICIOUS CHRISTIAN FRIEND. AND YOU CAN PRAY.

All these things you can do. You can persevere in doing them. And you have far more encouragement to set about the work, than you have to prosecute any secular scheme or business whatever.

Are you willing to make the trial? An eternity of joy or misery may hang upon your decision. What shall it be? Will you still neglect the great salvation? Or will you, in humble dependence upon the Spirit of God for all needful grace, begin at once TO CONSIDER THE SUBJECT OF PERSONAL RELIGION?

THE END.

www.ingramcontent.com/pod-product-compliance
Lightning Source LLC
LaVergne TN
LVHW050527100826
845148LV00002B/463

* 9 7 8 1 4 2 5 5 1 9 8 2 7 *